There is no substitute for a good reference book of strategies, d
ideas like those found in this book. Every modern option trader using fast on-line fills
and low commission rates - has to learn to rely on himself if he or she wishes to trade
with the confidence it takes to make money consistently.

Sing Systems
OPTIONSEXPOSED.NET

This publication is intended to provide training information and commentary on the subjects covered. It is sold with the understanding that neither the author nor the publisher is engaged in rendering legal, accounting, or securities trading, or other professional services. If legal advice or other expert assistance is required, the services of a competent professional person should be sought.

Any stocks or trades, observations, and opinions based on real or fictitious equities, are used for illustration and teaching purposes only in this book- and are not intended to be trading advice on any specific equities or products.

OPTIONS EXPOSED *PLAYBOOK*

THE MOST POPULAR AND PROFITABLE ONLINE OPTION STRATEGIES OF ALL TIME

BY DON A. SINGLETARY

- *Options Monthly INCOME – Learn to trade Credit Spreads low-risk , profit 10-20% in less than 30-days on risks as low as $250-$500 per trade.*

- **If you are already trading options and losing money, this could be the most important option book you will ever read.**

- **A 25 year trading veteran shows you how to trade smart and Option Selling to make regular monthly/weekly income.**

Plus you get a free download:
SPECIAL BONUS CHAPTER
with excerpts from *Options Monthly Income:*
3 STRATEGIES THAT WORK SO WELL THE PRO'S TRY to SELL THEM TO YOU

Using Powerful Online Trading Platforms
Accelerated Learning Techniques
Easy-to-Understand and Execute

OPTION TRADING DEFINITELY OFFERS WAYS TO INVEST SMARTER; YOU LEARN TO USE STRATEGIES WHERE YOU CAN HAVE MORE CONTROL OVER THE RISKS YOU TAKE AND USE LEVERAGED TRADES TO SAVE YOU MONEY AND PROVIDE OPPORTUNITIES THAT STRAIGHT STOCK INVESTMENTS CANNOT OFFER. THIS OPENS UP NEW POSSIBILITIES FOR TRADING, MANY THAT MIGHT NOT HAVE BEEN AFFORDABLE IN ANY OTHER WAY.

LEARN PASSIVE DIRECTIONAL TRADING WITH HIGH PROBABILITY OF PROFIT

Simple language and modern methods of learning option trading.

You get step-by-step basics in an OPTIONS PLAYBOOK with 30+ powerful strategies.

Options Exposed
PLAYBOOK
THE MOST POPULAR AND PROFITABLE
ONLINE OPTION STRATEGIES
OF ALL TIME

DON A. SINGLETARY

- You can use options to make money every month or every quarter.
- Learn to use Covered-Calls and roll-out strategies to decrease the cost basis of stocks in your tax-deferred accounts.
- Trading Options Online is one of the fastest growing segments for personal investors.

Plus you get a free download
BONUS CHAPTER on

"3 Strategies That Work So Well the Pro's Try to Sell Them to You"

–excerpts from the author's earlier *top-10 options eBook*

Contents

Preface

Why Online Option Trading, Why this Book, and Why Now?

If you've been considering taking an expensive course to learn to trade options, you should read this book first; it can save you a lot of money and time. The internet has totally revolutionized the way option trading is learned and executed. The online trading companies are now so advanced and competitive that they offer free and powerful software to attract new customers; the same software trading platforms and data that used to be so expensive only the pro's could afford them.

This book takes you quickly through the basics, and it's written specifically for individual investors who want to create income streams and who'll be trading online and paying the lowest commissions possible. The task of this book is to get you up and running, then lead you through the basics to becoming an intermediate level trader.

No matter if you are young or old, man or woman, technology is the great equalizer. All who apply are accepted immediately – and you can set your own pace as you learn lessons that can make you money for a lifetime.

I've been trading options over thirty years and I can guarantee you, there is no need for you to learn options the way I did. You won't have to wrestle with math and read hundreds of pages on formula derivations; this is a user friendly book with simple language that directs you to the very best and most modern (free) apps, videos, websites, and training in the world.

Technology now makes learning options easy. Before GPS, when navigating in the car - we had to unfold paper maps and stop and ask for directions if we got lost. Now, a little voice gives us directions while we view a real-time tracking of our pinpoint location. A similar thing has happened with options trading. What used to take weeks and months of study through hundreds of pages of probability statistics – is now done transparently by the online trading platforms – *the free programs you get when you open a trading account.* This book shows you exactly how to get all this and use it to learn options in the most modern and easy ways possible.

This is a book for of all types of investors - from *very conservative for retirement plans to strategies for the speculator.*   You'll also learn a technique the pro's have used for years – sometimes called *passive directional trading,* a strategy for income from options that works in bull, bear, and neutral markets.

If you have already traded options, and haven't been making money with them – this might be one of the most important option books you will ever read.

How to Use this Book

There are new ways to learn option trading: A majority of equity options trade online - and almost all individual investors use deeply discounted commission electronic accounts. Many books on options have fallen behind and are still teaching option trading as though it exists separately from online trading. **What is different about his book is that its purpose is to get you ready to open your online account and begin to trade options online. You can also use vendor and association supplied graphs, charts, videos, and articles for in depth study.** For those already trading options, we aim to help you up your game to more profits. This book covers generic information on basic options to advanced strategies that will help you with *any of the online trading platforms available.*

Once you open your account and install your free trading platform from your broker – you'll be joining the fastest growing segment of new online investors. One of the two fastest growing demographics are sharp young people that are technologically savvy who want to extend their skills into areas to help them find financial security. The other fastest-growing group consists of retirees - and those who have retirement in sight. These investors want to work a few hours a week and they expect to be paid well for the effort.

If you expect nothing but easy money, little work or effort, and that you won't have to take any risk, you will be disappointed; this is often called 'free lunch' – and it just doesn't exist. Option trading definitely offers ways to invest smarter; you learn to use strategies where you can have more control over the risks you take and use leveraged trades to save you money and provide opportunities that straight stock investments cannot offer. This opens up new possibilities for trading, many that might not have been affordable in any other way.

The goal here is to help you get a fast-start to opening your account and to begin trading with confidence. You'll study 30+ strategies with tips and ideas on advanced strategies. You will be guided to many free and unbiased resources to take your knowledge and trading to higher levels; this includes free mobile apps, videos, and the many training features of your online trading platform. We'll show you how to use paper-trading with live real-time info, so you can actually perform trades while you learn.

There is a special emphasis on spread trading; a common and advanced category of strategies often used to reduce risk. You will learn how to apply risk probability in your trading decisions. Spread-trading options allows you to design trades to fit your account size and risk levels – through the range from conservative to speculator.

Trading options successfully requires the ability for you to be ruthlessly honest with yourself. If what you try isn't making you money, you have to change it. The new online option software that your trading company provides takes time and practice to learn; this process is not unlike players who become expert at video games. You will be encouraged to use practice mode trading, sometimes called paper-trading. You'll want to explore the powerful features of your trading software provided to you free when you open an account; these are your tools for your new job of online option trading. Learn to use them or you won't make it. If you want to learn to trade smarter and are willing to do the work; you came to the right book. Thank you for your purchase; now let's get started and have some fun.

Casino operators make the most money from one game that is the simplest, requires no system, knowledge, or thought whatsoever: SLOTS

"I'm not a fan of people who say you shouldn't be doing this," said Thinkorswim's founder Tom Sosnoff of investors using complex strategies. "Imagine you walked into the casino and people said to you, 'You look stupid so you can only play the slots.'"

Welcome ladies! Here's a list of common option terms: call, put, spread, split, straddle, and strangle. For too many years, the 'men's club' has held the keys to the kingdom. Women are among the fastest growing groups of online option traders. – the author

Just because the market is open does not mean you have to trade. Cash is a position too.

Control your own destiny or someone else will.

Any trader can take risk, a great trader can do it with purpose and use it to their advantage.

1 Welcome to Online Option Trading

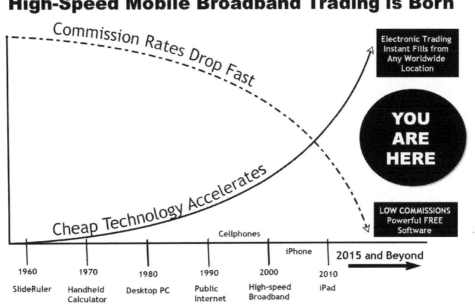

Every reader deserves to be lead straight to these lessons without excessive pep talks, and chatter of making easy money. Not three investors of a hundred understand and use option trading, even though they are a top investment tool. My job is to take you through the basics and speedily show you how to use spread trading and other advanced strategies that can keep you in your comfort zone while learning to harness and use some great trading techniques.

Options for Income

The surest, safest way to make option income money is to sell options. The very first strategy in this book is on writing (selling) covered-CALL options. Selling options on stocks you already own (or will buy) is a strategy so safe it is approved for use in self-directed retirement accounts. This strategy can easily add 5 to 10% or more to the returns on your account, and the strategy works in bull, bear, and neutral markets. In many cases, depending on how your money is invested, it can actually double the return on your retirement funds. Most people don't know about it, hesitate to learn more – and so are missing out on one of the greatest boons to personal investments of a lifetime. Once you learn this strategy and gain a little experience, it might only take an hour or two a month for you to significantly add earnings power in your retirement account. *This is the safest application of option trading that is available and also one of the most common and easiest.* This type of trading is considered smart and passive. Many fund managers use it all the time to increase performance in stock funds. If you own stocks, this is a great way to get your feet wet and gain some experience without significant risk exposure.

Sophisticated option strategies are available for all risk tolerance levels. One of the most valuable lessons you will learn about trading options is that they have a 'risk control' that is not unlike the volume control on a radio or TV; you can select from a range of risks and possible rewards. You not only select a strategy (type of trade), you also choose the risk level by choosing which *strikes* to use, and which stocks and market views to employ (tactical). For professional option traders, *option spreads* – not outright buying of PUTS and CALLS- are preferred trades and there is a reason for this: They are the trades that give you the most control of risk in trade selections.

The discussions of *Vertical Spreads* describe the most commonly used combination strategies by beginners and advanced traders. Investors who own stocks in trading and tax-deferred accounts will want to consider the covered call strategies, collars, and also techniques of rolling out covered options to increase return on equity in these accounts.

Protection and Hedges

In building financial wealth and security, making profits trading is only half of the task; the other equally important half is learning to keep the money you make. Wealthy investors actively use risk management techniques to protect investments, while surprisingly few individual investors with self-directed accounts are aware of these relatively inexpensive and easy strategies to protect the gains they have made. No one questions the necessity and wisdom of insuring their car, home, and life – but we are not commonly taught how to do the same by strategizing protection in our retirement accounts. Traditionally, financial advisors advise almost everyone to use what is called *asset allocation*; that is dividing your investments between categories like: stocks, bonds, real estate, precious metals, and other strategies. What often happens is that most investors have most of their funds in stocks, and when the market crashes and/or particular stocks fail, a great deal of hard-earned profits are lost. Many financial planners allow investors - and even condition them - to expect large losses as an inevitable part of their stock portfolio – and they are not totally wrong. What you may not know - is that sophisticated and wealthier investors will not tolerate that advice; when they have large gains - they understand the good practices of protecting their gains. The regular everyday well-meaning investors are also trained by many money managers and financial advisors to diversify, so 'when the market varies you won't have all your eggs in one basket'. "Spread the risks," they say - among dozens of stocks. In other words, if you buy stocks or other investments, adapt a passive attitude and learn to take your lumps and do nothing. You should seriously question this attitude.

There is a very popular investor who has ignored this advice for years and is one of the richest people in the world, Warren Buffett. There are some good books on how he does it and well-worth the read, but I am going to share, in my own words of course, what I believe to be the essence of this genius investor. What I admire most about Warren Buffett is that what he does is little more than common sense and quite logical, and yet it goes against virtually every money manager that urges people to diversify widely to avoid risks. I'll explain it right now in simple language and you make up your own mind: If you owned a stable of 100 thoroughbred race horses, and 10% of them won 95% of the races, why would you enter all 100 or even 80 of them in the races? You wouldn't! And that, my friend, is how easy it is to show you the essence of good investing. There is a current day movement among modern managers that is ditching the long-held -and perhaps overly simplistic view- of safety in diversification – and it's about time. This doesn't negate nor deny investing in various *kinds* of assets for safety, but if you are going to put money in stocks, you might want ten good ones instead of buying 100 with a shotgun approach. And when you do get those windfall profits, you might consider protecting profits instead of just passively letting it ride – as a strategy.

Learning to use options for protection is nothing more than choosing the right tool for the right job. It makes perfect sense to learn to make better choices about protecting what you have made. You took risks to make that money and it paid off; now *doing nothing* to protect it may be taking risk unnecessarily. Savvy investors know that *doing nothing* is a choice with consequences. If you made 50% profits in your account in five years, would you spend 1% of your profits to protect it? You probably answered 'yes'; options can be an inexpensive way to protect what you've already accomplished – and in the long run, keeping what you make will have you making even more. Anyone who learns to make money but fails to learn how to keep it, doesn't really understand investing; they only have half of the equation. A stock with a high beta tracks the larger market, perhaps mirroring the S&P 500 or another index; options on an index can be used to hedge profits. Have you ever plotted your retirement fund's performance against an index like the S&P 500? That's what one does to see if options on that index are a viable way of hedging your profits against downside sliding.

Using options on ETF's -*exchange traded funds* – that track major indexes like the DJIA or S&P500 is a great way to use options to protect you from poor stock market performance. Understand also, that this protection is not just an 'on-off' function but can be used to hedge to various degrees. It isn't just an all or nothing proposition. There are ETF's available for very specific market segments too, like petroleum, interest rates, or pharmaceuticals. Not all ETF's have options available.

Speculation

One of the major advantages available to option traders is *leverage*. Buying 100 shares of a $125 stock would cost $12,500 while buying the CALL option might be close to $800. In effect, you are controlling a large value of the stock for a relatively small amount of money. The stock shares are a risk in value equal to the purchase price, while the option maximum loss is the cost of the option only. Unlike buying the stock, the option purchase has an expiration date, so timing is a major consideration when using options instead of buying the underlying stock. And there are ways to use option spreads to reduce both the cost and the risks of speculative trades. You can just as easily find option strategies for bull, bear, or neutral plays.

The Attractions of Option Trading

The leverage: Controlling large assets with a small amount of money.
Flexibility: Being able to make money in any type of market – bull, bear, neutral
Risk Selection: Be in control of the amount of risk you take on any investment play.
Protection: Having economical ways of protecting money you have already made.

All of the above are great - but the thing I enjoy most about option trading is that I can open my office anywhere I can get an internet connection. My second favorite thing about trading options is the strategy of *selling* them. About 80% of options expire worthless; this means the odds are in my favor from the very start of these trades. As you read more about how this works, you will realize you can make money selling options even when your market view is wrong. You will learn how to use your online trading platform to measure the risk of each of these trades and to calculate the probability of profit of each and every trade. I didn't say it was easy and I didn't say you will always make money, but the smarter you learn to trade – the luckier you'll get!

I think a great many online traders of stocks, options, commodities, and other products – all share the fantasy of sitting under a palm tree at the beach being able to use our computer/mobile device - to make money. The idea of using our own resources and wits to pursue profits from just about any location at any time, is something that appeals to most women and men. Truth be told, I don't really need the beach and palm tree so much; I just enjoy the freedom and sense of achievement. And I have to say, being able to have the resources, the time, the opportunity - and the freedom and good health to do all this - is something I never take for granted. The third thing I love most about option trading is being able to share what I know with people and making new friends with like-minded people.

One common myth about trading options is that there are only a few types of traders. In fact, options offer so many choices, that you will eventually find the strategies and risk tolerance that will be a fit for you. We all have different tastes for food and our preferences in types of music – and you will also find what suits you best as you gain experience with options. There are plenty of strategies for very conservative types and for all speculators.

Contact Information

Only a few of every hundred investors understand options, so welcome to an elite group and congratulations for entering this group of knowledgeable investors. By the time you complete this book you will be among relatively small group who understand and undertake the strategies of option trading.

If you have any questions or comments, or if you find mistakes and would like to bring them to my attention, you will find my contact information at my blog at: **OptionsExposed.net**

I am always seeking ways to update and improve the information in this book. Thank you. My email address is: **Don@WriteThisDown.com**

2 Basic Theory: CALLS and PUTS

Options are contracts with obligations and rights.

An option is a ***contract*** to buy or sell a specific financial product known as the option's ***underlying*** instrument or underlying interest. For ***equity options***, the underlying instrument is a stock or an exchange traded fund (ETF). The option contract itself is very specific. It establishes a specific price, called the **strike price**, at which the contract may be **exercised**.

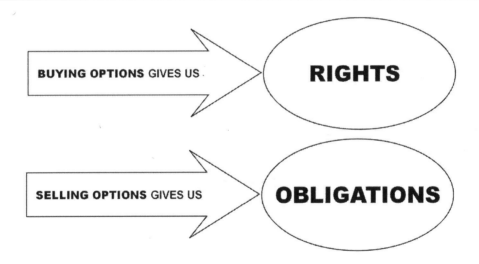

BUYING OPTIONS GIVES US — **RIGHTS**

SELLING OPTIONS GIVES US — **OBLIGATIONS**

BUY A CALL: The RIGHT to BUY at the strike
BUY A PUT: The RIGHT to SELL at the strike

SELL A CALL: The OBLIGATION to SELL at the strike
SELL A PUT: The OBLIGATION to BUY at the strike

Terminology

PREMIUM: An option's premium is the *price* of the option or the cost of the specific option. If you sell an option, you collect the premium for a **credit**. If you buy an option, you pay the premium for a **debit**.

In stock option trading, each option represents the rights to 100 shares of the underlying (stock). Option prices are quoted in cents per share and one option represents 100 shares.

For example: An option quote of 2.65, means $2.65 cents per share for one-hundred shares, so the actual cost of the option quoted as "2.65" is $265.00 ($2.65 x 100). In this case the premium (cost of the option) is $265. If you SELL the option, you get a *credit* of $265, and if you BUY the option, you have a *debit* in your account for $265.

The **STRIKE** of an option is the same as its STRIKE PRICE; these terms are interchangeable.

EXPIRATION, (aka: EXPIRATION DATE, DATE OF EXPIRATION) means the date the option contract expires. All options have an expiration date. The expiration date of an equity option is usually the third Friday of the MONTH for which the option is named. The MONTHLY stock option is the most common type; there are also WEEKLY options - meaning options that are shorter term than MONTHLY options. An equity (stock) option may or may not have options for every calendar month; the most common options are MONTHLY options. Many equities have both MONTHLY and WEEKLY options; it just depends on the particular stock. The MONTH of an option is signified by a standard three-letter capital abbreviation: JAN = January.

XYZ SEP 50 CALL AT $2.30

STOCK SYMBOL: XYZ **MONTH:** SEPTEMBER
STRIKE: $50 **TYPE:** CALL OPTION
PRICE: $2.30 ($230.00)

OPTION PRICING

In-the-money: commonly abbreviated as ITM

A CALL option is *in-the-money* when the underlying stock price is HIGHER than the strike.

Example: XYZ 50-strike CALL is in-the money when the underlying stock is priced HIGHER than 50.

A PUT option is *in-the-money* when the underlying stock price is LOWER than the strike.

Example: XYZ 50-strike PUT is in-the-money when the underlying stock is prices LOWER than 50.

Out-of-the-money: commonly abbreviated as OTM

A CALL option *out-of-the-money* when the underlying stock price is LOWER than the strike.

Example: XYZ 50-strike CALL is out-of-the-money when the underlying stock is priced LOWER than 50.

A PUT option is *out-of-the-money* when the underlying stock price is HIGHER than the strike.

Example: XYZ 50-strike PUT is out-of-the-money when the underlying stock is priced HIGHER than 50.

At-the-money: commonly abbreviated as ATM
When the underlying stock is priced at the strike price.

COMPONENTS OF AN OPTION'S PRICE

An option's price has two components the *intrinsic* value and the *time* value (extrinsic).

Example: XYZ stock is trading 52. The XYZ SEP 50 CALL is trading for 3.45.
The CALL is (52 minus 50) 2.00 in-the-money; this is its *intrinsic* value.
It's time value is 3.45 minus 2.00, so this option's *extrinsic* value 1.45 of the 3.45 total premium.

INTRINSIC VALUE

A CALL has *intrinsic value* when the underlying stock price is *above* the strike.

    Example: XYZ 50 CALL and the stock price is 52.35, then the intrinsic value is equal to the stock price minus the strike: 52.35 – 50 = 2.35 intrinsic value.

A PUT has *intrinsic value* when the underlying stock price is *below* the strike.

    Example: XYZ 50 PUT and the stock price is 46.30, then the intrinsic value of the PUT is equal to the strike price minus the stock price: 50 – 46.30 = 3.70

In other words, whether the option is a PUT or CALL, its intrinsic value is the amount it is in-the-money (ITM).

TIME VALUE

The time value is equal to the option's premium minus the intrinsic value. If the option is not in-the-money, it has no intrinsic value, so the only value it does have is **time value**.

Time value and implied volatility are the two major components of an *extrinsic* value. The longer time an option has until its expiration date, the greater the time value of the option. There is an attrition of an option's price (premium) that occurs as its expiration date draws nearer in time. This reduction in the options price due to this, is called **time decay**. Normally the time until an option's expiration is express in days, thus – you might see it indicated by (60) is it has sixty days until expiration. In trading monthly stock options, it is generally assumed the trader knows a MAR stock option will expire on the third Friday in March. There are also weekly (shorter term) options available on many products, and also LEAPS. These are Long-Term Equity AnticiPation Securities® (LEAPS®). These types of options are priced in a similar fashion as regular monthly stock options.

Quick Review: So far we have learned that *intrinsic value* is the amount (if any) the option is in-the-money. The other major component of an option's price is *time value* which includes some price based on the *implied volatility* (IV%).

IMPLIED VOLATILITY   or   IV%

The implied volatility (IV%) is subjective and it affects the time value portion of an option's premium. Volatility is a measure of risk (uncertainty), or variability of price of an option's underlying security. For example, the volatility of an underlying stock is a measure of the probability of the stock's price changing; this change may be in any direction at any time. *Volatility is the measure of an underlying's potential price change in any direction.*   Since the value of an option depends on movement in the underlying's price, a higher (assumed) implied volatility - portends more fluctuations (in either direction) in underlying's price levels.

The 'implied' in implied volatility reflects some of the value in an option's price - based on what the market (other traders) think it's worth. Having said this, there are parameters and events that warrant changes in implied volatility.   The IV% of the underlying can change for any number of reasons that influence the price of the underlying.   Even if you never learn to trade volatility, an advanced technique, every trader of options has to understand how it affects your trades.

Historical volatility refers to the volatility of the underlying stock. *Implied Volatility* (IV%) is a term that applies only to options.   These terms could be confusing if you are beginning to learn them. The present value and trend of an underlying's implied volatility are important in option trading. There will be some discussion of the aspects of trading IV% later in this book.

TIME-DECAY

One of the most valuable concepts in trading options is to understand time-decay in option pricing. Time-decay occurs at different rates throughout an option's life, and is accelerated as the option nears expiration, with the decay accelerating especially in the last 30 days. The much steeper slope in the time-decay graph as the options nears expiration represents this relationship.

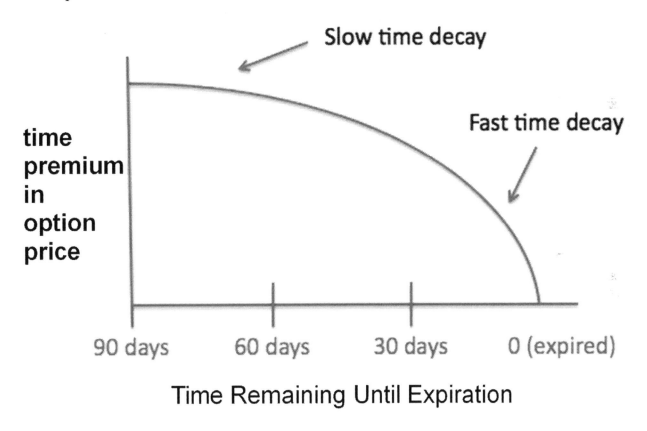

The LONG and SHORT of it: When you buy an option or stock, you are said to be LONG the product. When you sell a product (you sell when you did not own it), you are said to be SHORT. This SHORT is backed by cash in your account, thus 'cash secured' is applicable.

Over time, an option's premium will be decreased by its time-decay component. SHORTING or selling options by using combination trades called *option spreads* can be one of the most easy and successful – and less risky strategies in options trading. When you sell an option, your account is given a CREDIT; if that option expires worthless – you get to keep that money. This is sometimes called 'selling time-value.' You collect the option's premium – and if the option expires worthless (out-of-the-money with zero time value), you profit. When the option expires, it is taken off the trading board (gone or unlisted) and you simply keep the money you were paid when you sold it; you need do nothing further. Even with basic option trades, there is money to be made in bull, bear, or neutral price outlooks depending on which strategies you choose to play.

Using On-line Trading Platforms

As you trade options online, you will be supplied a trading platform by your vendor (broker). Until a few years ago individual traders would buy and use sophisticated and specialized options modeling software – and this software could cost from a few hundred to a few thousands of dollars. Now, you get the equivalent FREE when you open an account. These programs are electronic trading platforms that supply quotes, news, charts, graphs, helpful information – and a myriad of other services. There is a learning curve in using this software but you will find that these brokers also have excellent people and videos to help you. Some of these vendors have various versions of trading platforms; for example, they might have a full sophisticated version for advanced level traders and they will also have a more simple version for traders who just want to execute simple buy and sell orders on products. If your aim is to learn options properly, go ahead and choose the full version; learning how to use this powerful trading software is more than worth the time. You will still be able to use simple features and be able to explore and learn more as you get more familiar with the program – and remember, all these programs have support people you can email or phone to help you. Most of them also have free training videos.

Important Note for Beginner Level: You should be able to begin trading right away. There is no reason to feel you must master all the features of the software for online trading before you begin. To help you build confidence, most vendors allow you to operate in a practice or 'paper money' account. To start you can use this account, plus each vendor is very generous with phone help, text discussions of common questions, and free videos to train you on the software. All you need to bring is a basic knowledge of option strategies and terms. Options are not so complicated as many people believe; after you learn the basic terms and simple strategies, your learning will accelerate quickly. This new software is not only ideal for trading options, it will accelerate the learning curve for option beginners - and advanced students.

Option Premium Major Components

- Underlying Price

- Strike

- Time Until Expiration

- Implied Volatility

Interest rates and dividend payments and dates of those payments are relatively minor factors in option pricing.

Volatility, Standard Deviation, and Probability of Profit

You don't have to be a statistical math wizard to trade options, the software pretty much automatically does the heavy work for you. You will learn the common terms, concepts, and strategies - so you can learn to think in terms of *probability of profit*, which is what evaluating the possible merits of a trade and strategy is all about. These parameters allow us to gain a snapshot of a trade. We incorporate this with the other technical and fundamental information about the underlying - to arrive at our *market view*, which is our opinion about the magnitude, direction, and timing of price movement. Armed with this information, we are able to use the trading platform's features to help us analyze the viability of specific trades. This helps us form a *strategy*. Choosing the option classes, dates, and prices are the *tactical* decisions.

The graph below is simply the standard graphic representation for what is called the *nominal distribution of probability*, a symmetrical representation of what *standard deviation* means. *Nominal distribution of probability* and *standard deviation* are terms used in describing the probability used in option trading. Variations of three SD's (standard deviations) will comprise 99% of all most possible outcomes. The option trading software from your vendor uses this to compute the probability of the underlying's price movement in option modeling. Two SD's (standard deviations) represent 95% of price probabilities for a given time period, and one SD represents 68% of them. As option software computes these probabilities, it is actually running the figures for specific areas inside the curve(s).

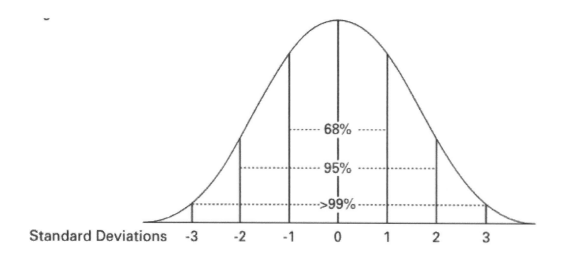

The slopes and relative areas of 1,2 and 3 SD's change according to the volatility of prices. Volatility is a measure of the likelihood and magnitude of price changes.

Here's a slightly simplified explanation of how the math works.   If a stock has a volatility of 20%, then in one year, the stocks price might be expected to vary up or down 20% of its price in one SD (or 68% of all possible prices).

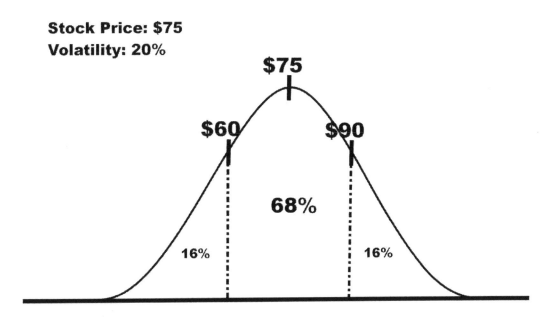

The trading software you will be using will use the underlying stock price, the option strike price, time until expiration, and the implied volatility to compute a mathematical probability of profit. The result is a number usually identified by **"Prob OTM %"** or **"Prob ITM%"**, respectively representing the probability the option will expire out-of-the-money and expire in-the-money. Many of these programs will take it a step further and will input the options price and commissions and compute the mathematical **Probability of Profit** for the trade – and often it will be displayed graphically. Advanced traders will learn how to perform this on several trades at once, so they may compare and select the best trade for a market view and strategy. In the graph above, one could surmise there is a 16% chance of the price in one year being either below $60 or above $90 per share. (100% minus one SD 68% = 32% and half of the 32% is on each extreme, the below 60 – and the above 90.

Remember, these results are mathematical functions and illustrate snapshots of probable price movement. This modeling does not include directional price bias; you will be doing that based on your knowledge and research for the underlying (stock, index, or other products). It does offer you the probability of the magnitude of a price change over a given period of time- with no directional bias at all.

Another notation here: Such charts as the one above use a *linear* nominal distribution of probability. Most of the computer modeling is done with what is called a *log normal* distribution of probability which is slightly more accurate. The reason for this is that although price movements of stocks have an unlimited upside, they do have a finite downside (zero) value. This causes the linear distribution to be slightly less accurate than the log normal distribution. The difference in most cases *is too slight to make much difference*; some of the software allows the user to toggle the methods. This fact is mentioned here so you can know the difference.

Basic Four

At the most elemental level, there are only four basic option trades. There are two kinds of options: CALLS and PUTS. And you either BUY or SELL them. Everything else is strategy and combinations of buying and selling more than one option at a time.

LONG CALL

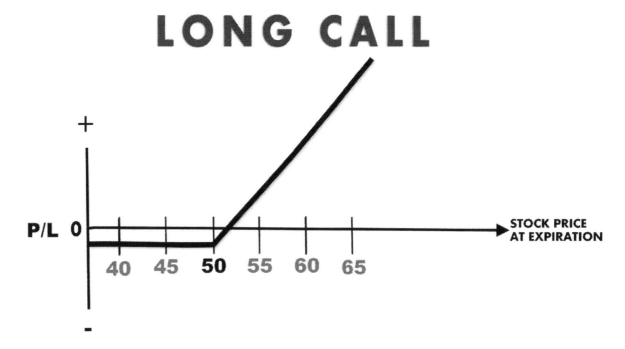

EXAMPLE:

BUY 1 XYZ 50 CALL

MARKET VIEW: BULLISH
IV%: lower, moving up

MAXIMUM GAIN: Unlimited
MAXIMUM LOSS: Price of CALL
BREAK-EVEN: Strike + Option Price

When you buy a CALL, it's time value is decaying – working against you. Ideally you buy a low IV% that is rising. Your goal is to have the value of the CALL increase as the price of the underlying goes UP.

SHORT CALL

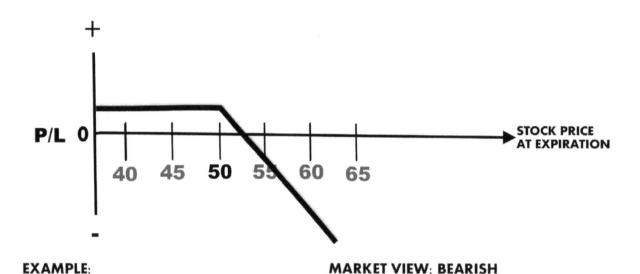

P/L 0 ———→ STOCK PRICE AT EXPIRATION

40 45 **50** 55 60 65

EXAMPLE:

SELL 1 XYZ 50 CALL

MARKET VIEW: BEARISH
IV%: high> stable or down

MAXIMUM GAIN: Price of CALL
MAXIMUM LOSS: unlimited
BREAK-EVEN: Strike + Option Price

When you sell a CALL, its time value is decaying, working for you. Ideally you sell with a high IV% trending lower, decreasing the value of the option.

LONG PUT

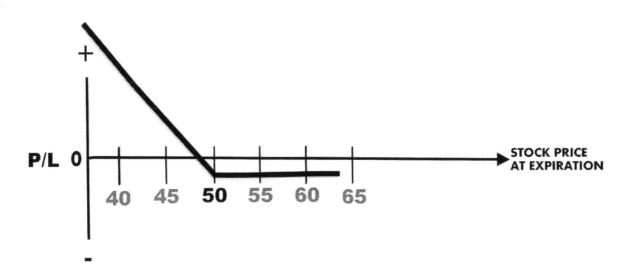

EXAMPLE:

BUY 1 XYZ 50 PUT

MARKET VIEW: BEARISH
IV%: lower & moving up

MAXIMUM GAIN: Strike Price - Option Price
MAXIMUM LOSS: Price of PUT
BREAK-EVEN: Strike less Option Price

When you buy a PUT, time decay works against you. You want a low IV% that could rise giving more value to your option. You want the value of the PUT to increase as the underlying goes DOWN.

SHORT PUT

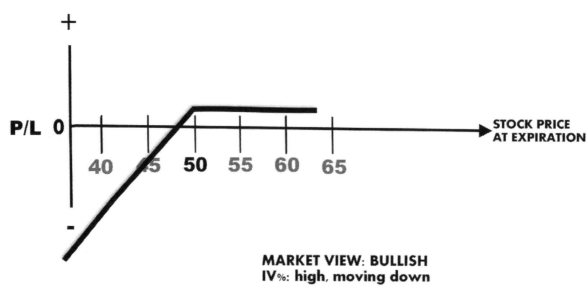

P/L 0

+

−

40   45   50   55   60   65

STOCK PRICE
AT EXPIRATION

EXAMPLE:
SELL 1 XYZ 50 PUT

MARKET VIEW: BULLISH
IV%: high, moving down

MAXIMUM GAIN: Price of Option
MAXIMUM LOSS: Strike - Price of PUT
BREAK-EVEN: Strike less - Option Price

When you sell a PUT, time decay is working in your favor. Your prefer to sell higher IV% and trend lower.

Characteristics of Options

Remember that each stock option contract represents 100 shares and the quoted option prices are in cents per share. Here is the **option chain** for Coca Cola CALL options and a **matrix** with information about the options.   Of course all the options and quotes used here will have been long gone by the time this book goes to press. Note the options have 80 days until expiration.

The CALL KO Matrix

This matrix of CALL option prices and other stats are for the KO (Coca Cola) JUNE 2015 (top) and the AUGUST 2015 (bottom) **classes**. The finely shaded boxes represent the ITM options. When you get online and trade with your vendor's software, you will be able to choose your own layout preferences and show any and all option parameters in customized screen layouts. In this table are shown the bid/ask, last trade price, delta, implied volatility (IV%), and the probability the option will expire OTM. Note the stock price at the moment this table was created was $40.51 per share.

		Symbol	Price			
Stock:	Coca Cola	KO	40.51			
CALLS	Class	Days until Exp				
	JUN 15	80				
Strike:	Bid	Ask	Last	Delta	IV%	Prob OTM
36	4.70	4.80	4.70	0.85	17.88%	19.87%
37	3.80	3.90	3.85	0.8	17.57%	24.60%
38	2.95	3.05	3.00	0.74	17.41%	30.92%
39	2.19	2.24	2.20	0.65	17.61%	39.06%
40	1.54	1.59	1.55	0.55	18.19%	49.34%
41	1.03	1.06	1.04	0.43	19.02%	60.52%
42	0.65	0.67	0.66	0.32	20.13%	71.34%
43	0.39	0.42	0.41	0.22	21.94%	80.40%
44	0.24	0.26	0.25	0.15	23.84%	87.01%
45	0.14	0.17	0.15	0.10	25.94%	91.55%
CALLS	Class	Days until Exp				
	AUG 15	143				
Strike:	Bid	Ask	Last	Delta	IV%	Prob OTM
36	4.80	4.95	4.85	0.81	17.69%	25.66%
37	3.95	4.10	4.00	0.76	17.68%	30.71%
38	3.20	3.30	3.25	0.69	17.00%	37.01%
39	2.48	2.66	2.52	0.62	17.74%	44.13%
40	1.89	1.95	1.92	0.53	18.16%	52.25%
41	1.38	1.44	1.40	0.44	18.81%	60.67%
42	0.99	1.03	1.01	0.35	19.53%	68.82%
43	0.70	0.75	0.72	0.28	20.72%	75.93%
44	0.49	0.51	0.50	0.21	21.78%	82.10%
45	0.34	0.37	0.35	0.16	23.16%	86.72%

The JUNE 15 class expires on the third Friday of June. This chart was made 80 days prior to that date, thus 80 days until expiration.

Study the option prices in relation to the various strikes that are 'in' and 'out' of-the money (ITM/ OTM). The AUG 15 class are slightly more expensive than the nearby JUN 15 class when you compare the same strikes for each class, reflecting more time value in the option prices for the AUG class. The IV% is used as an indicator of 'how expensive' an option is. The IV% is relative to each strike and class and is not an absolute value. Although they are not shown in this matrix, remember that theoretical values of options are probability based forecast on volatility and time, not directional indicators. On the other hand, the IV% can be used to imply both the underlying stock's volatility and often the implied likelihood of price movement. With experience, you will learn to glean the market's opinion of the likelihood of price movement in one direction over another by observing skews in volatility (deviations on *perceived value* rather than mathematical inference – the math being absent any opinions).

Study the Prob OTM in relation to the strike prices and the current value of the underlying (40.51). As the strike price is farther from at-the-money, the Prob OTM% becomes greater. Normally, a longer time until expiration has a less predictable movement of the underlying's price. The longer time until expiration, the more things that can happen, thus – less certainty.

Remember the components of an option's price: Price of the underlying, days until expiration, volatility of the underlying, and the strike price. (Dividend payments & dates, and interest rates are also factors in option pricing, but very minor when compared to the other contributors.) Of course the further OTM the strike from the stock's price, the higher the probability that it might expire without any intrinsic value. The next matrix is from the same day and time and it is for the KO PUT options for the classes of JUN 15 and AUG 15:

The PUT KO Matrix

With the underlying at 40.51, all the strike of 40 and below are OTM. Notice how the delta is -0.93 for the 45 strike PUT, and then drops off to -0.11 on the way to the 36 strike PUT. The 45 strike being deep in-the-money, while the 36 strike PUT is far out-of-the-money. Remember the delta on PUTS is expressed as a negative number, and delta for CALLS, a positive number.

Also note how the Prob OTM is greater the farther out-of-the-money the option strike is. Look on the table and you will see that ATM options have a delta near -0.50. Even the deep-in-the-money 45 strike has a delta near 1.0 at -0.9.

The IV% of one option price alone is useful, but the comparison of IV% at various strikes is where you are able to gain even more information. Often,

		Symbol	Price			
Stock:	Coca Cola	KO	40.51			
PUTS	Class	Days until Exp				
	JUN 15	80				
Strike:	Bid	Ask	Last	Delta	IV%	Prob OTM
36	0.21	0.23	0.22	-0.11	20.14%	86.90%
37	0.31	0.34	0.33	-0.16	18.65%	81.48%
38	0.48	0.52	0.51	-0.24	17.92%	73.59%
39	0.75	0.79	0.78	-0.34	17.22%	63.29%
40	1.15	1.17	1.16	-0.45	16.71%	51.22%
41	1.64	1.70	1.68	-0.58	16.17%	36.59%
42	2.30	2.35	2.32	-0.70	15.91%	26.93%
43	3.05	3.15	3.10	-0.80	15.86%	17.56%
44	3.90	4.00	3.95	-0.87	15.63%	10.45%
45	4.80	4.90	4.85	-0.93	14.86%	5.06%

PUTS	Class	Days until Exp				
	AUG 15	143				
Strike:	Bid	Ask	Last	Delta	IV%	Prob OTM
36	0.42	0.46	0.45	-0.17	18.52%	80.25%
37	0.59	0.62	0.60	-0.22	17.62%	74.28%
38	0.82	0.86	0.84	-0.29	16.89%	66.77%
39	1.14	1.18	1.16	-0.38	16.28%	57.91%
40	1.54	1.58	1.56	-0.47	15.58%	48.18%
41	2.05	2.09	2.07	-0.58	14.99%	37.98%
42	2.66	2.72	2.70	-0.68	14.47%	28.13%
43	3.35	3.45	3.40	-0.77	13.82%	19.12%
44	4.10	4.25	4.18	-0.86	12.61%	10.77%
45	4.95	5.10	5.02	-0.95	10.35%	3.29%

comparing the skews of IV% of both the PUTS and CALLS, can reveal by implication the market's opinion of the underlying's price direction, or can tip you off to look for more news on the stock. An option's IV% is normally higher - the more the strike is OTM. In the tables of these KO PUT's, the strikes of the PUTs at 40 down to 36 are increasing; the farther OTM, the higher the IV%.

Here's another term you need to learn:

The difference between the 'bid' and 'ask' is called the *gap*; normally the more volume an option is trading, the narrower the gap (just as in stock trading). A small gap means a more efficient (fair) market.

Delta

Delta is a theoretical estimate of how much an option's premium may change given a $1 move in the underlying stock (or other product). Delta may be the most important of the 'Greeks', so let's review to make sure you have an understanding of this term.

Example: (reference to the illustration of the matrix of the KO CALL options on page 23) KO is trading at a price of 40.51. The JUN 15 40-strike CALL last traded at 1.55 and has a delta of .55. This means if the underlying stock price varies by $1, the value of this option might vary about $.55. If KO increased to 41.51, the option price might move up to 1.55 + .55 = 2.10.

If you bought the option at 1.55 and it moved up to 2.10, it increased in value by $55. This means it increased in value to $210 from $155, a 35.4% gain.

Had you bought the underlying shares of stock at $40.51/ share, the 100 shares would require an investment of $4051 and the increased value of those hundred shares would have been $100 (100 shares x $1.00), or a gain of only 2.4%. The option trade is highly leveraged.

Buying the CALL delivered a *leverage* of about 14.75 times that of buying the stock outright. This is what is meant when we say options can be a **highly leveraged** investment. This example shows a gain, but never forget this is a double-edged sword that works the same high leverage on losses.

Go back to the KO matrix for CALLS and PUTS. You will find the PUT delta is expressed as a negative number; this is because the price movement would be downward (decreasing); the CALL deltas are always positive. The maximum value of delta is 1 and the values of delta are always between 0 and 1. As a rule-of-thumb, ATM (at-the-money) options have a delta of about .50. In-the-money strikes have higher than .50 deltas. Out-of-the-money strikes have a delta between .5 and zero. Of course the delta of an option changes all the time; the more towards ITM, or deeper- ITM an option becomes, the higher it's delta. And inversely, the further the underlying's price moves away from a strike, the lower the delta will become.

Delta is an important term that you will use a lot. Later when we study compound option trades (using more than one option in a strategy), you will discover that simply algebraic adding the individual deltas of the option *combinations* you use, will give you the **net delta** of your compound trading strategy position. You will also discover how combining options can dampen or desensitize a strategy's price or volatility movements; this is one of the ways advanced traders can use strategies to fashion a tactical option play.

For now, keep it simple. None of us learn advanced trading techniques before we capture the basics. The good news is that it is easy to use the basics and to be able to make profits. Options are not so much complicated as they are just unfamiliar; getting fluent using common option terms takes practice, just as learning anything does. There are two types of options, CALLS and PUTS and you either buy or sell them. It is the coupling of your option knowledge with your skills at reading the possible price movements of stocks that will make you money; the two are inseparably linked.

I am often asked why there isn't more about selecting the underlying (stocks) for option trading in this option book. Learning how to choose good stocks is a vast subject. What is unique and adds new dimensions to option trading is that you can trade regardless of whether your view on a particular stock (in a fixed timer period) is bullish, bearish, or neutral. It takes practice and experience to become confident in the selection of trades and the subject is too vast for any one book. I do post articles with some examples of how I select some option trades in my blog at OptionsExposed.NET. I hope you can find some help there as I discuss apply option strategy to a stock price scenario. Watch and read about how various option traders link strategy and an underlying. You will find a wide variation in methodology. By your exposure to new ideas on trading, you will naturally – over time-gravitate to the types of trades suit your risk adversity and account size.

Stock profits are mostly a simple linear function. You buy low and sell high, or sell high and buy low. Options give you dozens of more choices. To make money on a stock, you must be right about the direction of price movement, the magnitude, and the timing of that movement determines the amount of your profit. It is possible and actually quite common to make money using option trades without having to be correct about predicting price movement of the underlying. This is the 'magic' of trading options. This is only half of the good news! In the next chapter, you will learn the equivalent of opening your own casino and you can sell options to high risk takers - and usually keep their money --- that is what casinos do! You get to choose whether you want to be the speculator (high risk taker) or the house (low risk taker), whether you want to figuratively, own the casino or be the gambler. Learning how to trade smarter can make you profits on a regular basis without taking a lot of risks. Plus you will learn how to use *covered call* options in tax deferred accounts to give some boosts to your savings plans; this is one of the option strategies so safe it is approved for use in those types of accounts.

3 The Amazing Covered CALL Strategy

Learning the basics of option trading is now easier than ever. Anyone can get fantastic option trading software (aka: trading platforms) free from their online trading company. After studying up on the basics, using the paper-trading account is one of the best and speedy study methods. Here is a very low-risk simple strategy that is probably the most popular of all option trades; the **covered call**.

An investor who owns stock (or who will buy it) can write (sell) options on an equivalent amount of stock and collect the premium income *without adding additional risk of additional liability (there can be an opportunity cost)*.

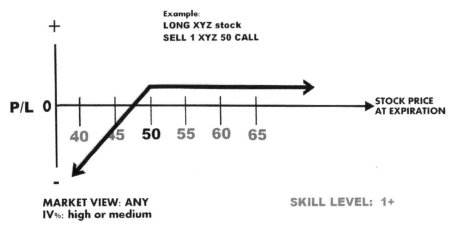

If you own a stock (or buy it), you can sell a covered CALL option with a striker higher than the stock price (an OTM CALL) and the premium is credited to your account. If at option expiration, the stock is below the strike, the CALL expires worthless and you keep the credit. If the stock is at or above the strike of the CALL option at expiration, you are obligated to sell the stock at the strike price. What you risk is any gains you might have made from the sale of the stock *above* the strike price (aka: opportunity cost).

COVERED CALL example:

Scenario: You own 100 shares of XYZ that you bought at $40/share six months ago. Suppose that stock is now trading at $48. You might be able to sell a 50-strike CALL that expires in 30 days for a premium of 2.50.

If you hold both the stock and the short CALL until expiration AND the stock is trading at $50 or above – the stock will be 'called away' (the CALL option is exercised) at the $50 strike price. When you sold the CALL, you became obligated to sell the stock at the strike price of $50, if the option was exercised. The net result is that you profited from the stock gains and you collected the premium of the CALL. 2.50 + 50 less cost of of the stock at $40 = net profit of $1250, $250 more than if you had just held the stock to sell at $50/share; that's an 'extra' 25% (250/1000).

If you hold both the stock and the short CALL until expiration AND the stock is trading *below* the 50 strike at expiration, you collect the $250 premium and you still own the stock at whatever price it is trading at that day.

Very few options are exercised unless they are ITM at expiration, but you should understand that a CALL option can be exercise *at any time during the contract* (through the expiration date). If this had happened, you keep the option CALL premium credited to your account and you are obligated to sell the stock at $50. You do not incur any further charges or commissions.

 The investor doesn't have to sell an at-the-money call. Choosing a strike price simply involves a tradeoff between priorities. You sell a higher strike if you are very bullish on the stock.

The covered call writer could select a higher, further out-of-the-money strike price and preserve more of the stock's upside potential for the duration of the strategy. However, the further out-of-the-money call would generate less premium income, which means there would be a smaller downside cushion in case of a stock decline. But whatever the choice, the strike price (plus the premium) should represent an acceptable liquidation price.

(You could also buy back the short CALL at a loss – and/or 'roll it out'. This will be discussed in subsequent text.)

Consider timing: If you own a stock and are expecting a price rise soon, you could regret losing the stock during a price rally; this is a consideration before selling a covered call. If you write a covered call and the price rises unexpectedly and you wish to hold on to the stock, the only way out is to buy back the CALL – and this would likely cost you; at least some of the loss would be covered by the call premium you collected.

The great thing about writing (selling) a covered call is that the investor can choose the strike price; normally a strike price OTM (above the stock's current price) is sold. As more distant (higher) strikes are sold, the amount of premium you collect will decrease.

Another potentially very important consideration is the tax you might have to pay. If you have a large profit in stock you are holding, then you could owe substantial taxes if it is 'called away' (the short call is exercised). You should seek tax advice if you are at all in doubt of what you might owe. This is assuming you are not writing covered calls in a tax-deferred account. Since there are no tax consequences in a tax-deferred account, the covered-CALL strategy is ideal in this type of account.

Selling Covered Calls in Tax Deferred Accounts Can Be One of the Best Strategies

Most self-directed tax deferred accounts are allowed to use the COVERED CALL strategy; not all brokerages, trading companies, or custodians allow it. You have the right to move your account in most cases or to ask to change the restrictions. Of course whether you should or not - is not within the scope of this book. Having said that, selling covered calls in tax deferred accounts is quite common and done all the time.

Selling covered CALLS in tax-deferred accounts is one of the safest and most dependable ways to increase an investors return from 5%, 10%, or more annually. Many investors have stocks in these accounts that pay dividends, and also the stock's price rises over time. Selling covered calls on these and other stocks can simply add another source of income.

Selling Covered Calls can make money even when a stock price: Goes up, Remains the Same, or Goes Down

The investor usually selects a strike OTM (above the stock price) to sell. If you are selling calls on a stock that you have in the 'long term hold' category (meaning you are not thinking of selling it at this time and are holding it for (more) long term gains, you may simply sell a CALL far OTM, and collect the premium. In the case of such stocks, the investor who has owned it for some time – has likely been paying attention. The investor is familiar with potential earnings, earnings reports, trading ranges, price volatility of the stock, and in many cases - the investor follows news on the stock for months and often years. In other words, if you were a hunter, you could say you 'know this animal and his habits very well.' If the investor has stocks like this, or even if he doesn't own it yet and is very familiar with it's price behavior – then that stock could be a good candidate for the covered call strategy – also sometimes called 'the covered write'. Understanding a stocks range of trading is key to choosing covered call strategies. If the investor can select a call strike to sell that the stock is not likely to reach – and think the premium of selling the call is worth the additional risk, then this investor will likely keep the premium in all these three cases: the stock goes up, but not above the strike, the stock price remains the same, or the stock price goes down – and the investor doesn't mind continuing to hold the stock (staying 'long').

There is a very important parameter in your trading software to help you make decisions; it is 'Prob OTM.' This can be shown in your trading matrix for a stock's options and it literally means "the probability this option strike will be out-of-the-money on the date the option expires."

The example used is here is only for illustration; by the time you read this all the parameters will have changed and the options expired. Since we just used the KO option matrix for CALLS, it will be used here again (the table on page 23). This time we'll be using the matrix to examine possible strikes to sell using the 'Prob OTM' parameter. We'll examine the option premiums for various strikes, and then we'll discuss some choices. The objective of this example is to take the reader through a typical scenario and to discuss some considerations when selecting a call option to sell.

Remember this stock is currently priced at 40.51 per share, the JUN 15 options are 80 days until expiration, and the AUG 15 class expires in 143 days. Notice in the one-year chart KO is 40.51 and has traded near 45 twice in the last twelve months and is currently only about 3.5 dollars from its low of the last year near 38. KO is the type of blue-chip stock that many retirement portfolios choose to buy-

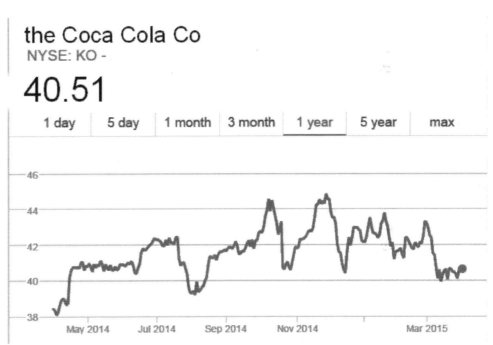

the Coca Cola Co
NYSE: KO -
40.51

| 1 day | 5 day | 1 month | 3 month | 1 year | 5 year | max |

and-hold. From a technical standpoint there seems to be price resistance near 45 and significant price support just above 40. KO has been trading in a defined range for at least the last six months. None of this takes away from the view that KO is a good long-term buy-and-hold investment.

It isn't always the thing to do - but in this example, we'll choose to sell a call from the JUN 2015 class; the reasoning being that there seems to be more certainty about price behavior in the next 80 days, than in the longer AUG 15's 143 days until option expiration.

This is a good time to point out the difference in the 45 call options prices between KO **JUN** 45 CALL, priced at .15 ($15 each) and the more distant KO **AUG** 45 CALL priced at .35 ($35 each).

Now you are ready to hear about a perfectly boring trade that will make you money and generate income on a regular basis. As you view the matrix, you could be thinking that because of KO price behavior of the past year, the KO stock probably won't trade above a price of 45 within the next 80 days. Look at the price of the KO JUN 45 CALL and you will see the market agrees with you; the price is bid/ask 0.14/0.17 and the last trade is at .15. Also you read in the Prob OTM column that there is (at least) mathematically a 91.55% chance the option will expire worthless (meaning you keep the premium and your KO stock will not likely be called away (or ITM). Now you must determine the true viability of the trade: Will it make enough money considering the low risk of the trade? Of course,

Stock:	Coca Cola	Symbol	Price			
		KO	40.51			
CALLS	Class	Days until Exp				
	JUN 15	80				
Strike:	Bid	Ask	Last	Delta	IV%	Prob OTM
36	4.70	4.80	4.70	0.85	17.88%	19.87%
37	3.80	3.90	3.85	0.8	17.57%	24.60%
38	2.95	3.05	3.00	0.74	17.41%	30.92%
39	2.19	2.24	2.20	0.65	17.61%	39.06%
40	1.54	1.59	1.55	0.55	18.19%	49.34%
41	1.03	1.06	1.04	0.43	19.02%	60.52%
42	0.65	0.67	0.66	0.32	20.13%	71.34%
43	0.39	0.42	0.41	0.22	21.94%	80.40%
44	0.24	0.26	0.25	0.15	23.84%	87.01%
45	0.14	0.17	0.15	0.10	25.94%	91.55%

CALLS	Class	Days until Exp				
	AUG 15	143				
Strike:	Bid	Ask	Last	Delta	IV%	Prob OTM
36	4.80	4.95	4.85	0.81	17.69%	25.66%
37	3.95	4.10	4.00	0.76	17.68%	30.71%
38	3.20	3.30	3.25	0.69	17.00%	37.01%
39	2.48	2.66	2.52	0.62	17.74%	44.13%
40	1.89	1.95	1.92	0.53	18.16%	52.25%
41	1.38	1.44	1.40	0.44	18.81%	60.67%
42	0.99	1.03	1.01	0.35	19.53%	68.82%
43	0.70	0.75	0.72	0.28	20.72%	75.93%
44	0.49	0.51	0.50	0.21	21.78%	82.10%
45	0.34	0.37	0.35	0.16	23.16%	86.72%

each one of us has different risk adversity, investment philosophy, and risk tolerance. Now, let's do the numbers on this trade. Let's say we intend to consider selling ten of the KO JUN 45 CALLS at a price of $15 (.15) each for a total of $150.00 credit from the options premium.

Of course we must consider a number of things. How much commission will we have to pay to sell ten of these options? Commonly, online accounts are charging from 65 cents to $2.00 per option. Obviously, if you use a full service broker (*financial representative* they are often called), it might cost you $10 or more per option – and there's no way you can pay $10 each to trade a $15 option – 2/3 of your credit would go to paying the commissions and your risk versus reward is skewed past common sense and good money management. (Please remember this book is for low commission online investors using free vendor provided software. This doesn't ignore or discount the value of a good broker/consultant and $10 is a perfectly reasonable commission for trades handled in person by a live broker instead of trading electronically.) I am pointing out that you can place trades with very low commissions, that are just not practical when paying $10 or more per side or 'each way'. (each way means 'in' and 'out' of the trade).

In our example, I will use not the lowest or highest commission rates of online trading, but will use something in between that usually doesn't require a huge deposit or minimum number of trades to maintain. The commission rate used in this example is $1.50 per option on each side of a trade (you pay $1.50 to buy and/or sell it 'each way').

Selling 10 of the KO JUN 45 CALLS will gain us a credit of $150 minus (10 x $1.50) a $15 commission, a net credit in our account of $135. Remember, since you own the stock you are not required to put up any margin (deposit) to make the trade; you are selling 'covered' calls, meaning the stock is the collateral for the trade.

So how do we know this trade is worth it? I know plenty of investors that wouldn't give any consideration to a trade that only has a maximum $135 upside. One could sell ten of the 43-strikes for .40 and collect $400 - $15 commission for a net credit of $385, and the trade would have a 75.33% chance of total success. I am using the more conservative example choice here and I'll tell you why. Many, certainly not all, of the readers of this book are new to option trading; they want to tread carefully until they are more comfortable with all the new terms and have more experience trading with the software their vendor has provided. If you are already confident and your goals and risk adversity can tolerate more risk, that is your choice. I have learned from teaching and talking with new option investors that most of them prefer to take things slowly until they build up more experience and confidence. I don't judge; that's not my job – but it is my advice to neophyte option traders to take things slowly until your confidence builds. Make some lower risk trades, follow along, get used to the terms and software. Even many experienced traders might be new to low-commission online trading methods. Most traders will be successful at learning their own limits and abilities over time; I urge you to trust that.

The example of selling those ten KO JUN 45 CALLS is the **covered call** strategy – and does require you either own or buy the underlying shares; since each option represents 100 shares, it takes 10 x 100 = 1,000 shares of KO in your account – and trading at $40.51 per share they are worth $40, 510. In no way is it realistic to expect most new option traders to have that kind of resources for only one trade (although a great many do). For this reason, I'll include a second example here; an example that dollar-wise is not a large risk, but it won't require a large amount of capital either.

Let's assume you own 100 shares of KO, worth $4,051. Go back to the KO JUN 15 matrix and consider selling one of the KO JUN 43 CALLS for .40 or $40. After the $1.50 commission, you net $38.50 and you still have the Prob OTM of 80.40%, pretty nice odds. If you tell a friend you are learning to trade options and just 'made $38.50' by clicking your mouse or tapping the screen two times - they might not get very excited. After all $38.50 isn't much money. Remember, the purpose of these types of trades, would be what I call 'training-wheels' trades; use them to learn, gain confidence, get experience. Learn to trade smart and understand all you can about the risks of option trading. My way of looking at it is not that "I only made $38.50 for clicking a mouse a few times" but to think of it as "getting paid to go to school." I happened to have used KO in this example, but you might consider the strategy using a stock you already own of course.

I promise it will be worth it in the end for you to put in the time and effort to gain the knowledge and experience. Many options traders, a great many actually, do jump in over their heads - and when they lose money doing it, I assure you they rarely tell everybody about the mistakes they make. Far more than half the people working in this country don't make $38.50 an hour and you already know how to make that much in only five minutes! That's a rate of $462 an hour. I would say that is a good rate to be paid 'while you are learning'.

Trading these low-commission, small transactions online is an ideal way to learn; the dollar amounts are relatively small. The type of trade just described is pretty low-risk, and you can do small trades like this with several different stocks at once, then track them all and learn! And you get to do it all privately in your online account; this privacy is actually very liberating and allows you to learn faster.

There are great rewards for learning the skills, math, theory, investment methods, strategies, and even the patience it takes to be a good trader of options. Yes, patience is a valuable commodity; not everybody has it or can get it. Patience is like experience, you learn it over time - you will be paid very, very well for learning it.

GAIN THE KNOWLEDGE   DO THE WORK   TRADE SMART   MAKE THE MONEY

Another Great Advantage of Selling Covered CALLS

Since selling covered calls is among the most conservative and relatively safe option strategies, it has an inherent advantage to all investors learning to trade options: Trading covered calls has almost all the components you need to learn about trading options. You will learn option pricing, how to use your vendor software to study individual option parameters, you'll become familiar with terms, you learn about time-decay, how to compare option prices and classes, about using Prob of OTM and Prob of ITM computations, and you get to do all this while not exposing yourself past your risk tolerance.

How to Reduce Your Cost Basis in Stocks
by Continuously Selling Covered Calls

As you sell covered calls, if you choose wisely - you will profit more often than not. As you gain experience with selling those calls, you also will continue to learn more about specific underlying stocks and their price patterns and trading ranges.

When you sell covered calls on underlying stocks that you own (or buy), as they expire and you collect credits from the premium, it will definitely occur to you to keep doing it. Many times after you've sold one covered call and it becomes relatively worthless (a good thing as you have sold it, not bought it), you will have little to gain by waiting for the little amount of premium left to decay completely, so you can buy it back – for much less than you sold it for – keep the profit, then sell another option farther out in time. This process of closing one position and simultaneously selling another option is called *rolling out*. As you continue to roll out, this strategy will continually reduce your cost basis in the stock. Over long periods of time, these profits can add up – and it might only take you a few minutes each week or month to maintain these trades – and all the while you are continually making money.

Another example of rolling out short calls is when the underlying stock rises above the strike you sold - and to keep from being assigned (you are obligated to sell the stock), you need to close the position. As you do this, buy back the calls you sold (at a loss) by 'rolling out'. You may choose to roll out; that is to cover the ITM short call, and simultaneously sell a call *farther out* in time and with a *higher strike that is OTM*. This way you get to keep the stock, and although you might lose money initially as you roll out your short call position, you can continue to sell covered calls over time to increase your net profits.

Here's an example of rolling out:

You wrote a covered call on XYZ stock when the stock price was $47.50. You sold a nearby OTM 55 call option, and before the option expires the stock goes up to $57.25. You have made significant gains in the rising stock value for sure; more than enough to offset the loss of having to buy the 55 call back to close the position at a higher price than you sold it for (a loss). You may go out another three months or six months in time and sell a higher strike, a 65 for example and collect the premium. This is *rolling out the position*; in this case it might be called *rolling up* to a higher strike, and *out* to a more distant month.

The stock gains have been much more than the loss when you bought the 55 call back to close your trade – and you continue to write covered calls on the underlying stock you own. Buying the 55 call back (to close the position) insured you would not be assigned at the options expiration. ('being assigned in this case with a short call would mean you would have had to sell the stock at the strike of 55.) What you have lost is most of the gains your stock made above the strike price (55). This is because you had to buy back the 55 strike for more than you sold it for to keep from selling the underlying stock.

No matter how good you are at trading options and stocks, remember nobody has 100% winners. Part of keeping your momentum going is to realize this. Don't let having a few losing trades bother you; competitive people often have problems accepting any losses but they are a part of the process.

There is a saying among poker players, "Scared money never wins." If you are trading and always preoccupied with potential losses, you are likely trading out of your risk tolerance and/or your resources limits. If you have the resources and time to trade and do not enjoy it or find it too stressful - you must either quit trading, find a lower risk which you can tolerate, or consider finding someone who can help you with your investments. Everybody loves to make money trading, but not everybody has the risk tolerance or the resources to avoid 'trading scared'. It's only human that when people are outside the limits of their risk tolerance, fear keeps them from making rational decisions. Remember, it is not rational to expect 100% winners even though it is logical to strive for that.

The Most Common Mistake in Trading

This is a no-brainer and you already know all about it, but it might be good for you to hear it again – that's up to you. The most common mistake in trading is also the most common mistaking in living. We take our profits too quickly and let the losses run until we lose a lot. This is not only the worst mistake of investors but also the most common – and one of the hardest to cure. If you want to avoid it and you don't have an iron-strong self-discipline and a photographic memory – then you need to learn to apply discipline to your trading. This means keeping notes and records of how you are doing, so you can look at the results somewhat objectively. Doing this without fail - will help you learn faster with fewer mistakes. I know some traders, and I have done this myself, who make notes in the margins about 'what they were thinking' as they chose and placed a trade.

The reason for this most common mistake is that we must admit we were wrong to close a trade which we probably thought was a sure winner. We are put in a position to disagree with ourselves, a position that all of us naturally try to avoid. This is self-denial at its worst;

we must remember everyone has losing trades, disappointing trades, and there are times we don't recognize our mistakes until we have already entered a trade – and then irrational thinking can take over and increase what would have been tolerable losses. Every great warrior with a long career knows when he or she has to sometimes retreat to be able to fight another day. Keeping your money is just as important as making it. We normally like to think of ourselves as having a positive outlook and a life full of hope. Not learning to cut your losses, admit when a trade isn't working, and accepting the fact that you can't control everything - can lead to the quick end to your trading. Insisting on being hopeful on trades that go wrong - is a very bad habit – and it gets very expensive.

A disciplined trader knows when to exit a trade; it is a part of every trade to have a plan for all outcomes. One of the most wonderful things about trading is that it is solitary and we live and die on our own wits; that is also the worst thing about trading. Without discipline, very few traders are lucky enough to survive. Making smart trades is half of investing; the other half is learning to keep what you make.

Recommended Study Activity: Get to an internet connection or use your mobile device and conduct these exercises as a review for the material covered so far:

Go to your APP Store for mobile devices and download the OIC free app. OIC is an unbiased (no sales messages and a neutral view) source of very professionally presented lessons and information on options of all kinds and all strategies.

Log on to: OIC at **http://www.optionseducation.org** There are many similar sites with similar names - that are *not* the OIC website; *make sure* you have the **Options Information Council** before continuing.   Use your visit to OIC to:
    a) Find the Glossary of Terms: While there, review definitions to common option terms.
    b) Explore the section (see top menu of the web page) called: **Strategies & Advanced Concepts,** from the drop-down menu, select **Strategies.** You will see a list of strategies; click on one any one of them and you'll get a fantastic one-page illustration complete with definition, a graph, and simple, to-the-point guides to help you understand them.
    c) On this OIC website, they also have free videos, web seminars, and a completely free option training program.

Here's a question I get a lot: If all the info on options is available free from OIC, why do I need your book?
That's a very fair question. OIC is supported (funded) by exchanges, boards, and other industry agencies to provide training material to promote option trading of virtually all kinds. I recommend them because they are the greatest option training tool available anywhere, and it's organized so logically and done in the most professional manner possible. All the information you must understand is there in graphs, charts, videos, and even free lessons. This book offers guides and opinions not found on these types of sites. Think of this book as your tour guide to talk to you about experiences you can expect, and some insights on how you might find your own ways to think, trade, and explore all that can be done with options for an individual online trader. There is a lot of technical material on options, more than enough to last a lifetime. This book is to help you make the transition from learning about options to learning to trade them online using low-commissions & powerful software platforms. In my opinion, OIC provides the most organized, easy-to-navigate site anywhere to help you learn quickly, the basics you absolutely must have to trade options. (And they don't pay me to say that.)

Sing Systems

OPTIONSEXPOSED.NET

Free articles, trading tips, and option ideas at our blog: OptionsExposed.Net/blog

4 Selling Naked Calls and Puts

If selling covered calls is the most conservative of option strategies, then selling naked CALLS and PUTS *can* be called one of the most risky. One big crash market day that slams you can put an end to your trading account. There are a few conservative techniques that will be described here such as using option shorts to help you execute conditional trades where you want to put up the cash to buy or sell stocks.

Selling a 'naked' option simply means selling an uncovered option; you are not long or short the underlying but your deposits (margin, aka: funds in your trading account) are collateral for the trade. (naked = uncovered). The terms *uncovered* or *naked* apply only to *selling* options, not to buying them. The reason is that, unlike long options where only the price of the option is at risk, selling options (short uncovered options) can have in theory, virtually unlimited risk.

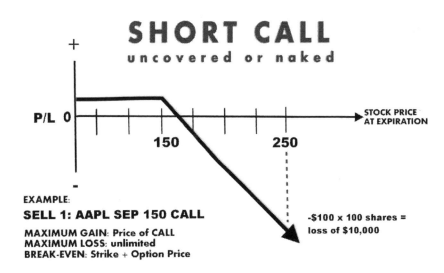

SHORT CALL
uncovered or naked

P/L 0

150   250

STOCK PRICE
AT EXPIRATION

-$100 x 100 shares =
loss of $10,000

EXAMPLE:
SELL 1: AAPL SEP 150 CALL

MAXIMUM GAIN: Price of CALL
MAXIMUM LOSS: unlimited
BREAK-EVEN: Strike + Option Price

Here's an example of how that could happen: Suppose you sell a CALL on AAPL (Apple stock), AAPL SEP 150 CALL and the price of the AAPL stock is $125 at the time you sell the CALL. If -prior to or at expiration- the price of AAPL goes to $250 a share, you lose (250-150) $100 x 100 shares = $10,000. Since the underlying has an infinite upside price - in theory, your potential losses are also infinite. If you didn't have that money in your account, you get a 'margin call' from your trading company (broker); this means they want money to be put in your account immediately or you must close the position. Truth is, your account is 'marked to the market' each day and during the day --- and you would get a margin call immediately if you didn't have the funds in your account to cover the required deposit for trading.

Conversely, selling a naked (uncovered) PUT has a similar downside risk. Here is an example: Sell the 100-strike PUT option when the price of the underlying AAPL is $125, and the stock goes to zero, you would lose 100 x 100 = $10,000.

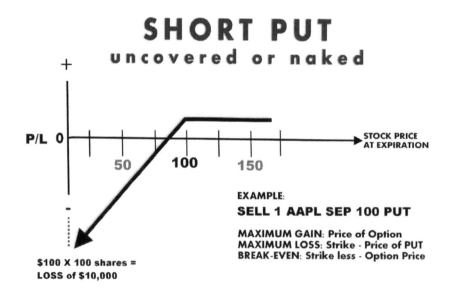

In reality, I would never advise anyone to sell naked CALLS on Apple stock; it is one of those long-term buy-and-hold stellar performers. It is also very unlikely AAPL shares would go to zero since the company has almost 200 billion dollars in cash reserves. Intelligent investors with common sense understand the distinction between *possible* and *probable*. Just because something is possible, is no reason to fear it. It is possible that on your next walk around the block that satellite debris could fall on you and kill you, but it is certainly not at all probable, nor should merely the possibility of it have you spending the rest of your life in fear of it. In option trading, we must know the possibilities to compute the 'worst case' and 'best case' scenarios, but we absolutely must understand how to use our software to glean the probabilities of a trade. Our trading platform is our control center.

The log-linear computations of your online trading software are going to automatically compute Prob of ITM and Prob of OTM percentages of each strike for you, and most of the online programs can even offer you a graph of price probabilities of an underlying (stock). *You must remember that these numbers do not have any bias about whether the price moves will be increasing or decreasing.* The IV% you read in option chains *can* reveal the market bias of a stock price; for example when you see (all other things equal) the CALLS or more expensive (higher IV%) than the PUTS – the market bias is bullish, and vice- versa when the PUTS are more expensive. You learn to add your research on the underlying stock to your decisions about buying or selling options.

Here's an example of combining the software's Prob of OTM with a market view of an underlying stock:

Suppose XYZ stock is trading at $75. Let us also in our hypothetical case - suppose you think the DJIA (Dow Jones Industrial Average) and the underlying stock price are both trading at the top of their ranges. I also recommend you rarely if ever trade options without knowing the earnings estimates expected and the dates of earnings reports (which can immediately influence stock price); dividend (payment) dates can also be a factor. Given these parameters, you might consider selling a far out-of-the money (OTM) CALL option. Selling this CALL will place a credit in your account for the premium of the option and you will have the possibility of unlimited losses. To compute the probability of the underlying stock price going higher than the strike of the CALL you are selling, you look for Prob of OTM% of the strike in the option matrix. Let's suppose you sell an 85 CALL that is 45 days from expiration and that the Prob of OTM% is at 88%. This means the straight math (no market bias) based on the stocks volatility indicates you have an 88% chance of making a profit and about a 12% chance of the stock being at or above the strike at expiration. If you have done good research and perhaps have followed this stock for a long time, you may have confidence that the stock price will not exceed the strike price of the option you shorted (sold). This means you likely have a greater than 88% chance of your option not being ITM at expiration. The worst case scenario is you are assigned short shares of the stock and have a risk the stock could rise and increase your losses. In most cases, the trader would buy the short option back (at a higher price than for which it was sold) and take the loss – prior to expiration.

In this hypothetical scenario, you are very likely (never certain) to make money whether the price of the stock goes down, remains the same, or even goes up – so long as it doesn't exceed the strike price at expiration. When you sell options, especially uncovered/naked options, you must have the mathematical odds in your favor and also some sound rationalization behind your market view. In selling a naked CALL, normally you use a strike well OTM. You trading software will give you the Prob OTM of all the available strikes, so you can shop them.

Theta

Theta is a function of premium time-decay; the higher the theta, the faster the option's premium decreases. Theta is represented in an actual dollar or premium amount and is usually calculated and display as the value for the current trading day. Theta represents, in theory, how much an option's premium may decay per day with all other things remaining the same.

Example: XYZ stock is trading at 80, the XYZ DEC 90 CALL trades at 2.35 and has a theta of .05 This option can be expected to lose .05 off its premium in a day due to time decay. If you are short 10 of these CALLS and theta is .05, then – all other things being the same – you can expect the value of the ten options to decrease by (.05 x 10) $50 a day.

If you are buying an option, you might shop options with a low theta, and conversely – if you are selling an option a higher theta would indicate a faster rate of premium decay. Time decay is not linear: During the life of an option, the rate of its time decay increases as it is nearer to expiration, so it's theta might increase (all other things equal), but as the option is very close (a few days perhaps), the theta can decrease because the value of the options extrinsic value is nearing zero. Remember theta is not the rate of time decay but the amount. Extrinsic value is the portion of the premium not caused by being ITM (IV% value and time value).

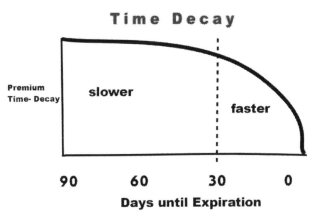

The slope on the time-decay graph indicates a faster drop off of time value in the last 30 days of an option's life. Since theta is the daily amount the premium atrophies due to time-decay, the value of theta generally goes up as the option nears expiration. This is precisely why option sellers wishing to collect premium from time-decay prefer shorter term options (fewer days until expiration, or the 'nearby' class of an underlying's options – sometimes called the *front month*). This does not negate the importance of a having a market bias or viewpoint when selling options, but many times when the underlying's price may go up and down, the time-decay is still on-going.

There are two good reasons the seller of an option prefers to short far OTM options:
1) There is less probability the option will expire ITM or be called away (higher Prob OTM% than ATM, ITM, and nearby strikes).
2) Almost all of the option's premium value is time value (the other major component is IV%).

Other Strategies Using Naked Options

I should have named this section "Getting Paid for Doing What You Were Going to Do Anyway". This is based on an actual trade I made just yesterday. I will call the stock XYZ, the actual name of it for the reader is not important.

About two years ago, I went to a breakfast meeting with friends and a new face was there. I introduced myself and in the conversation over the next hour-and-a-half - I found his son is a major operating officer in a company that handles financial products, mostly life insurance, disability insurance, and also buys and sells mortgages for homes and business. He was very bullish on his son's company and he told me the value of the stock was only around $5.00 share. Many traders won't trade stocks under $10 per share, others draw the line at $5; I prefer to at least listen and make my own decisions. When I got home, I bought a few hundred shares of the stock after reading the earnings reports and other light research; my feeling was that I wasn't risking much money. What locked in my decision is that the stock has a *book value* of $38 per share. The book value of a stock is how much money per share they would have if the company (in theory) closed it doors, went out of business and then sold off all its assets at current value and paid off all its debt. I am over-simplifying a bit, but book value is what the stock might be worth is the company drops dead. Since I was only paying around $5 a share, I felt the long-term risk was probably not high.

Over the next six months, the price of the stock doubled and I sold it at around $10.50. The stock went on to gain value up to $18 a share in another four months, but I remained quite happy with my 100% profit in six months. This is what is called 'plain old good luck'; I, nor anyone else, could have predicted with total accuracy that the stock would double in six months. My philosophy on what to do when I get lucky can be explained in only three words: "take the money". When the stock dropped back down to $14 dollars a share, then down to $12 share, I bought it back at 12.00, then sold it a week later at $14.00; this time I only made 16.66% in a week. I exercised my philosophy of good luck again and I 'took the money'. Over the next year, I wasn't as lucky; I didn't lose the profits I had made but I didn't make any more either – so I quit trading the stock and moved on to other things – but I always kept it on my watch list to see every day.

Just yesterday, I saw the stock trading down around $7.35 a share. I thought to myself, "If it gets down to below 7.00 I will buy 500 shares and plan on holding it. I checked and the book value was still near 40.00 /share. This stock is not traded nearly as much as any blue chips stock but does trade around an average of over five million shares a day. I checked to see if the stock had options and it did, but they are traded very thinly. When an underlying or an option trades 'thin', this means it is trading a relatively small amount on any given day. Option traders, normally avoid thinly traded options. When an option or stock trades 'thinly' the gap between the bid /ask prices often widens – and if you have to get out quickly, it can cost you dearly (because you can't get a fair price). This means it isn't trading enough to be in an *efficient* market. One can buy it one minute, sell it back right away and lose money- simply because their aren't enough trades/demand to have it trade at fair prices, or even theoretical values. Because of this reason, I did not want to do an outright options trade on this stock. In fact the 7.00 strike PUT only had 150 OI (open interests, the total number of all open trades on that option). Then I looked on the PUT matrix and saw that an option expiring in only 43 days with a strike of 7.00 was bid at .50. I promptly sold five of the PUTS with a strike of 7.00 for .50 each, and got a (5 x $50) credit, $250 in my account.

Now one of two things is going to happen: These options expire worthless if the stock is above 7.00 at expiration, OR the stock price would drop below 7.00 and I'd be assigned the 500 (5 x 100) shares at a price of $7.00, and since I collected .50 on premium, my net cost for the shares would be $6.50 per share, which is .85 below the stocks current price. This strategy is often called 'selling cash-secured PUTS'.

In other words, I wouldn't hesitate to own those shares at 6.50 and they are trading 7.35 now. So I would have bought the shares gladly at 6.50, so "I got paid for doing what I would have done anyway." And now, I won't be obligated to own the shares until (unless) they drop in price. I enjoy these types of trades 'to get paid what I would do anyway.' I fully expect those options to expire worthless. The margin requirement (deposit money in my account) to make the trade was about $840, and I'll probably make $250 on the trade in 44 days – a 29% gain. That is an annualized ROI (return on investment) of about 146%, not shabby! If I'm wrong about options expiring worthless, I will own a good little stock for 6.50 with a book value of almost $40. It is only fair to hasten to point out that these trades are never quite as easy, simple, or reliable as they may seem; I have had many of them go South on me. It's worth saying again "Nobody wins them all' and another adage that also holds very true over time, "There ain't no free lunch."

Years ago, the popular Will Rogers used to get a lot of laughs when he talked about investing in the stock market. He would say facetiously, "Buy low and sell high; if they don't go up, don't buy'em." I thought of those words as I placed the trade I just described, as it might be as close to taking his tongue-in-cheek advice as I'll ever get.

More Getting Paid for What You Would Do Anyway

If you have a stock in your portfolio that you want to sell but you are not in a hurry to do so – you probably have a target price in mind just above where it's trading now. It is just human nature to want that 'little bit more'. Well there is a way to sort of 'have your cake and eat it too.' Write covered calls on the stock and use a strike that you would be happy to sell the stock. The result will be one of two outcomes, and you win in either case. The stock is called away at the strike as the price rises to or above the strike price, OR you keep the premium from selling the OTM call and the net result is that decreases your cost basis for the stock. The only thing you 'give up' is any gain the stock might have made above the price where you would have sold it anyway! If you are the type of investor that would get upset with any of these results, don't do the trade. There are two other sage sayings: "There's is always 20-20 genius in hindsight." and "There are bulls, bears, and pigs!" *You must fully understand the best case, worst case, and probable outcome of each trade before you commit.* You will never be able to predict the future with certainty but you can understand and accept the consequences of each trade you choose to execute.

The Well-Rounded Options Education

One of the goals of this book is to help you learn to think laterally. The more you practice recognizing and finding opportunities in option trading, the better your results will be. Investors who think that buying only CALLS and PUTS is trading options, have missed the point. Sure, there are times when just simply buying a CALL or PUT may be just the thing to do. Experienced option traders who have earned an intermediate or advanced understanding of option strategies will learn to think in many directions at once, not just buying and selling, or even just making 'conditional' trades: "If the price goes above the strike, I make a profit. If not, I lose the price of the option and my risk is limited."

The simple and inexperienced way to shop options is to think "I'm going to buy some CALL options and try to make some money." You should be looking for investment opportunities and then knowing enough about various option strategies will gain you the advantage of finding (designing) trades that allow you to make the play with a high degree of success, ample leverage, lower risk, and worth the time and effort to make the trade. Many beginners will pick a strategy and then look for the investment opportunity; many times, this works just fine. I am saying that you should learn to think in other dimensions also – like when you see an investment opportunity, you know enough about options to find the strategies that will fit your goals, money management, discipline, and budget.

You must remember that most options are already fairly priced, you rarely find options truly cheap or overpriced that you can just buy or sell, although it does happen. Risk and gains are commensurate. When a stock is more likely to rise in price than decrease, its CALLS will be more expensive than the PUTS (usually a higher IV% will tip you off). There are some investors that 'value shop' options; that is they look for skews in implied volatility and hope to find a risk versus gain advantage due to some temporary imbalance. In the days prior to computerized/electronic trading, not all investors had access to the same quality information – and it may have been easier to value shop in those days. There were times when only those with access to expensive computers and software could glean that information – and for a number of years, these traders could scalp money that way by trading skewed option pricing. The good news now, is that any small account individual trader has access to the same information that professional traders do. These technical innovations have delivered a pretty level playing field among traders of all sizes, all the more important that your options education be sophisticated enough that you see far beyond merely buying and selling PUTS and CALLS. You gain an edge in finding more opportunities because you have an understanding that is broader and more useful than the average equity trader, or the average option trader. You simply have more tools, so you can find the right one - to do a better job.

Like equity trading, option trading is not a zero-sum game. One doesn't make money simply because another investor loses it. Your only competition is yourself. The goal is to learn and gain the experience to make smart trades that fit your own risk tolerance and goals or as I like to say:

- Gain the knowledge.
- Do the work.
- Trade smart.
- Make the money

5 Opening Your Online Trading Account

The application process is very simple. The brokerage company will have you fill out a few forms to open the account, execute a (separate) margin agreement, and you will add an options agreement to your account. These applications will gather information on you to make sure you are credit worthy and that you have the experience and understanding to trade your account at the various levels they may approve.

When a person opens an account, they are assigned one of several option approval levels supposedly based on the option trader's knowledge and needs.

In many instances, option traders opening an account are either not aware of these levels, or they will not be sure which levels they may apply to trade. After reading and studying this book, you won't have any problem going to intermediate levels. Experienced investors often qualify for all levels when they open the account, whether they intend to trade them initially or not; this keeps you from having to do more paperwork later, when you do wish to trade them. Anyone who is uncertain of their option approval level should read more about it (at OIC), or contact his or her broker to find out which level of option approval their account has.

Normally, there are four option approval levels. There is no official standard of what strategies could be traded at which level. The categories described below are typical levels used by most trading companies. A level 4 can trade all four categories, a level 3 can also trade 1 and 2 but not 4, and so on.

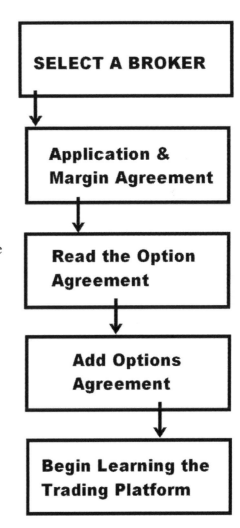

Option Approval Levels	Strategies Approved
Level 1	Covered Call, Long Protective Puts
Level 2	Long call/put
Level 3	Spreads
Level 4	Uncovered or Naked

If you only want to buy CALLS and PUTS, and sell covered CALLS, a margin agreement is not required. If you want to place debit and credit spreads, you'll need to have the margin account. To trade more advanced strategies, the brokerage company needs to know you have the experience and financial resources to trade these higher levels. After reading this book, you should have the knowledge many people need to get to the intermediate level trading.

You should read the technical brochure carefully – *Characteristics and Risks of Standardized Options* and make sure you understand the risky aspects of this type trading. You shouldn't have any problem understanding this brochure and the options agreement once you have read this book.

It is, by law, the brokers responsibility to gather this information on your financial resources and trading experience; most use a group of standardized questions on the applications.

You can read more about the LEVELS at the OIC.com website if you wish. Understand which of these levels are suitable for you before you apply for the account so you can communicate clearly with your trading company.

6 How Online Trading Increases Your Chances of Success

"Everybody is ignorant, just about different things." – Will Rogers

Learning is about changing our perceptions and being able to see new possibilities. Anyone who has the drive and interest to learn something new can do it so long as they have an amount of innate ability and some confidence to go with it. There is a notion, an antiquated notion I think, that people have to take long classes of study in things to learn them; this is like waiting for someone else's permission before learning a thing. With the internet and Google, there is no reason to wait to learn a thing anymore. For a long time, so-called financial professionals, including financial planners and brokers had specialized training and access to information that was not readily available to the so-called average person. Before the internet, people either had to phone a stockbroker's office or look in a newspaper to get a stock quote and if they wanted to put in a live quote machine in their office or home, it would costs hundreds of dollars a month. This was around 1990, twenty-two years after the CBOE (Chicago Board of Options Exchange) was opened in 1968. Now, all these things are as close as your cellphone, tablet, or PC – and they are free! You needn't wait for anyone's permission to learn a thing.

The lower cost of online trading presents new opportunities: Suppose that XYZ is trading for 48, and the XYZ SEP 55 CALL is selling for .40 and there is an 88% chance of Prob OTM. You can sell ten of them for a credit of (10 x $40) $400.

If you are using a full service broker (aka: financial services consultant) and you are paying $10 per option per side, it will cost you $100 to open the trade, and if you close the trade before expiration, it will cost you another $100 to buy them back (a 'closing purchase'). That $200 is 50% of the possible profit.

If you make the same trade online yourself, the commission per option per side (buy is one side, sell is the other 'side' of the trade), will likely be between 65 cents and $1.50, so both sides of the trade might cost you commissions between $13.00 and $30.00. That would be (13/400 or 30/400) from 3.2% to 7.5% of the $400 credit.

In this example: Using the full service trading would not only cost you half your potential profits, it actually makes the trade more risky. Paying $200 round trip (commissions on both sides of the trade), means if the CALL price decreased by 50%, you would only break even.

If you pay only $1.00 per side per option commission and the CALLS you sold for .40 - go down and you buy them back at .20 to close the position, you have a net profit of: $180 $400 initial credit, less $20 commissions, less the price of buying back the CALLS ($200) to close the position = net profit of $180.

Comparing the $10 versus the $1 rates, you can easily realize that if you had to pay a round trip of $20 per option- instead of only $2, you would probably select different trades. The higher commission rates can prevent you from participating in some low risk trades due to the higher expenses. Due to the lower commissions of online trading, you can make trades now – that were never available with higher commissions. Electronic trading has revolutionized option trading!

This is a good time to bring up another point: Why do you suppose I chose to use the example that closed the position on the short CALLS when the option premium went down to 50% of its initial value? There are thousands of online option traders that take those naked CALL option profits at 50%; it is their *plan*. Others decide to use a rule of the premium going down to 25% and hold the trades with that goal. What you decide to do is up to you. If you have lots of experience already, you have been through the mental process. If you are new to option trading, you need to know that it is quite common to have these sorts of self-imposed trading parameters.

In practice, there are many factors to take into account, and you won't go by *only* the option price. If the underlying tracks an average like the DJIA or the S&P 500, you could choose to ride the tide (ebb or flow). Sometimes company news on the underlying, or an unexpected buyout or merger, or other factors may show you good reasons to hold the trade longer (or not).

You should be warned that not every firm that presents themselves a *discount* broker is truly offering the best commission prices for trading. It is actually quite common for some online brokers to have a rate schedule of commissions that works on a sliding scale commensurate on the volume of trades you do in a month or year. There are 'discounts' and there are 'deep discounts'. Never be afraid to phone your online customer services and tell them you want to keep your account with them and in order to do that, you need to have the lowest commission rates you possibly can. You may be quite surprised what you get just by asking politely for it. If they refuse you when you call, you can move your account – or if you want just make yourself a note to call them back in a month and remind them how much you still need the lowest rates possible. Do not be shy about this. Remember, the lower your commissions, the lower the risk of your trading; the more of your profits you keep! If you have a friend with an account at the same company and gets low rates, tell them you know what he pays and you want the same rate.

There's another great thing about trading online that isn't discussed much. When you are alone at your computer studying matrix of option prices, doing research on the underlying, or even having to stop to find definitions of a new term or acronym – you can work at your own pace. Every piece of information and all the option parameters and prices are literally at your fingertips. Realize that your online broker not only supplies you with expert level software but they have free videos, telephone assistance, downloads to read and study, and most have regular free online webinars on how to use their software for specific purposes. These webinars are often recorded, so you can watch them on your own schedule. Many of us like to find our own answers by digging around; this is a good way to learn even more than you set out to learn. If you begin to get frustrated because you can't find just the right piece of information, stop and either text-chat or phone your trading company for help. They employ dozens of people who specialize in every important area of investing; they are usually quite eager to help you. Most trading companies have a dedicated number for their option help line; keep this near your trading desk. If people didn't need their help, they wouldn't have jobs! Use them. There is never a reason to build up unnecessary frustration or to put off learning something you need to know.

One piece of advice for when you do phone for help: Get right to the point and state clearly what you need. Especially during trading hours, time is valuable to these people and they are there to help, not to listen to people's 'stories' or experiences. When using brokerage help lines, it is good etiquette to be as accurate and brief as possible. Speak clearly and then listen; if the help operator – who likely has years of experience more than you do- uses terms or slang that you do not understand, politely let them know. They will take the hint and customize their replies to give you exactly the help you can understand and use. If you get information and need to think it over - or need to stop and study some points in detail, get off the phone and call them back later. Also have a pen in hand to take some notes. If the phone help operator refers you to a video, ask them if they can email or text you the link; this will save you time and it is easy to do most times.

If you ever do have to phone in because your internet goes out or any other reason that requires you to verbally give your broker an order over the phone, you must give your order accurately –and ALWAYS have them repeat it back to you. This is an absolute necessity and it is also common practice to keep errors to a minimum. You will rarely if ever - need to do this, but remember this tip. Never, ever be shy about making sure your order instructions are accurate; the trading company people that assist you - totally understand this and prefer you make sure everything is accurate.

Margin Requirements

The *margin* or *margin requirement* is the minimum equity (security such as stocks and/or cash) required to support an investment position. To *buy on margin* refers to borrowing part of the purchase price of a security from a brokerage firm. When you open an account (or modify an existing one) and *open a margin account*, you will approve an agreement (usually a separate agreement in addition to your account application) to put up assets in your account to use as collateral. Your account will be charged interest when your transactions use this feature. This interest rate is very low and usually is indexed to the prime rate – so will vary. For now, know that *margin* in the following examples is referring to the amount of equity (money or equivalent marginable security) required in your account in order for you to place a trade. Commonly, this may be expressed in your account details as *option buying power, stock buying power*, or other similar phrases. If you have any questions about how this works, you should contact the customer service at your trading company.

Here's an example of how the margin requirements are computed (all automatically in your account). Keep in mind that interest rates and requirements vary from time-to-time:

Sell five uncovered CALLS on XYZ Corp.
Deliverable on each contract: 100 shares of XYZ
Price of Security: $54.25
Market Strike Price: $60
Options Premium: $1.20

    Based on 20% Calculation
    Percentage of stock value:
    20% x [54.25 x (5 x 100)]   = $5,425

    Out-of-the-money amount
    (60 – 54.25) x 500   =   -$2,875

    Current market value of Options
    $1.20 x 500   = $ 600

Total Requirement   = $3,150

Hint: If you want to get a better feel for how much capital various trades require, just go to your trading company's software and go to the *paper trading* mode and then put in some sample trades; the amounts of margin required for various trades will be computed and displayed automatically. If you can't find it or need clarification, call their customer service for more information – and they can answer the specifics of your account if you have any questions. Knowing how to find and understand this information is vital.

By using the paper trade simulation mode of your account, you can accelerate your learning curve on both learning about options - and learning to use the powerful features of your vendor's software. Having real-time quotes, real configurations, and instant Greeks and stats and being able to compile any name trade is the absolute fastest, most accurate way to learn option and stock trading. There are literally hundreds of videos and a plethora of training material - all at your fingertips. Remember to get the OIC app for your tablet or cellphone and you will always have it to read and learn.

Reading is great to capture basics and to plan where to go next in your trading education, but real hands-on trading using the paper trade simulator is the only way you can learn how it all comes together. The difference is as much as reading about driving a car - and actually doing it; there is no substitute. You will learn at least five times faster by hands-on manipulation – than just reading about doing it. The goal of this book is to supply a sort of learning map, tips for showing you the way, and to open your thinking to the many possibilities ahead.

Seminars, workshops, forums, books, and trading groups all help stimulate ideas and possibilities; these introduce you to new ways to think and trade. But in the end, you will be back at the keyboard (or mobile device) and you will be using your vendors powerful software trading platform to execute your research and trading. Invest time in learning to use the powerful and analytical features of this software. The interactive visual nature of this software has a much wider learning bandwidth – than merely reading facts and calculating numbers. These interactive graphical features have the potential to teach more in an hour than a full day of reading, although the methods compliment each other. They supply you with a learning platform that is customized to your abilities, interests, and speed. Having these tools provided to you FREE, is the most liberating advance in trading in a hundred years; no other generations have ever had these resources. Anyone who tells you the way to learn options that does not include these resources is giving you outdated information.

Using Online Scans for Stocks

When you decide on your online trading company for options, it might likely be an existing account where you already trade stocks. Keep in mind you can open multiple accounts with the same broker if you prefer. Call customer service and simply explain to them what you want; most times they will easily accommodate you. If your present broker has competitive rates and trading platforms, it is easier to get familiar with one platform, than to try and juggle several of them. If you have an existing account and are adding the ability to trade options and/or additional accounts, this would be a good time to ask for the lowest, most competitive rates they offer. Many times, they will give you a lower rate to keep your business, even if you do not meet other requirements such as a 'minimum number of trades' to qualify for the lowest rates possible. If the particular operator can't help you, ask for a supervisor or department head who can make the decision.

In this section, I'll outline some of the most prevalent parameters that online software trading platforms offer. Taking some spare time on a regular basis to explore your trading platform will pay off for you. There is no need to try and learn it all at once; start with the minimum necessities, then explore by checking to see what training videos your broker offers. Put a reminder on your calendar to check for new features, videos, and other training information at least every two or three months; you will never regret doing this.

Stock Scans

By *stock scan*, I mean the search feature of your trading platform. You can put in parameters and have the software sift through thousands of stocks and deliver a list to you in seconds. (They also have option trade scan modes.) The terms and availability of the scans vary slightly from one vendor to the next, but you should know that all these features are normally included free in your software; the exception might be to an independent third-party investment service that your trading company presents to you. I suggest you get familiar with all the free features first, then shop advisors later; many times you can do research yourself instead of paying additional. Some of these services are very good and can save you time, but choose them carefully. The following scan parameters are common for stock scans and are a part of the online trading platform your trading company/ online broker provides free to you:

BASIC:
>Market Capitalization – The total shares outstanding and value
>Sector, Industry or Category
>Beta – How well a stock's price tracks the overall market fluctuations
>Index

FUNDAMENTALS

Revenue Growth/Loss
EPS Growth
Return on Equity
Profit Margin
Institutional Holdings

VALUATION

Debt to Capital
P/E ratio
Price to Earnings Growth
Price to Book
Price to Sales

DIVIDENDS

Dividend Yield
Dividend 12 month totals
Dividend Frequency

PRICE AND VOLUME

Current Price
Gap Up/Down
Price Change
New 52-week High/Low
Volume Range
Today's Volume vs. Average

TECHNICALS

Moving Avg. Crossovers
Bollinger Bands ®
RSI Relative Strength Indicator
MACD

Stochastic

(and scores of other technical indicators)

RATINGS

Buy/Sell Ratings, some for fees to buy third-party ratings

RESEARCH

Most trading companies provide information from their own in-house advisors. Follow a few of them and find a favorite to put on your reading list.

I would urge you to think of these SCANS as one of many tools and not something that you can tweak and then 'set and forget it' to pick your investments. Scans can save you hours of work, and you can even modify and save various scan parameters, each with specialized searches- and you re-use them again and again. Millions of online investors use such scans everyday. The best computer of all is still the one between your ears. You will also discover that your software has option scan features.

Lateral Considerations for Finding Trades

Sometimes a valuable part of learning something turns out to be *unlearning*. With options, you can trade bad news, good news, no news – so you need to learn to think that way. When I watch the financial channels, read articles/blogs, or follow up on a conversation with another investors – I make a note. Sometimes a scribble on a piece of paper, a voice note or notebook entry on my cell phone--- anything really to remind me to follow up.

One very interesting area is to check out the ETF's (Exchange Traded Funds). These can target groups of stocks, sectors of the economy, and other special interests and index-like functions. Options are available on many of them.

7 PLACING ONLINE ORDERS FOR VARIOUS TYPES OF OPTION TRADES

The free software, your TRADING PLATFORM, you get   when you open your account makes easy work of option trading. You'll be viewing the option quotes and stats on your underlying and can custom configure you screens to show various parameters and/or toggle back and forth among the pre-sets.

The best way to learn your software is dive-in; use the paper trade practice mode, watch selected videos and instructions on how to use

Your Trading Menu for Options

ORDER TYPE DROP DOWN BOX

Single
Vertical
Back/Ratio
Calendar
Diagonal
Straddle
Strangle
Covered Stock
Colar/Synthetic (Combo)
Butterfly
Condor
Iron Condor
Vertical Roll
Collar with Stock
Double Diagonal
Unbalanced

Screen Display Choices

Last X, Net Change
Theo Price, Mark
Volume, Open Interest
Impl. Vol, Probability OTM
Delta, Gamma, Theta, Vega
Position, Intrinsic, Extrinsic

SELECT PRE CONFIGURED
OR
CUSTOMIZED AND SAVE YOUR OWN

it. When you get stuck, call/chat for help. These software trading programs are very sophisticated and they have many specialized features that you might never use; you will become proficient at the features you use. The free video training usually has very targeted presentations. You might make an initial contact with the training staff and ask them which of these videos will help you target what you need to know. For example, you might tell them you know basic options and are interested in how to place *equity option spread trades* and how to use the program to chart those trades. You might tell them you own stock and you are interested in placing covered CALL strategies, or maybe you want to get instructions on how to display option data on your trade screen; this is one of the first things you'll want to learn. Also ask where you can download (for printout) the manual for the software.

Get to know your trading platform as an interactive teacher; it is a vital part of your option-trading education. For beginners, it is often best to have several distinct resources. For your familiarization with option basics through advanced strategies, I would urge you to get familiar with this website and organization: OIC (Options Information Council) at **http://www.OptionsEducation.org** I can't say enough great things about the material they provide. You can get quick, direct, accurate, information whether you are searching terms or want more details on a specific strategy. The way they present the information is nothing less than fantastic; you are always one-click away from clear one page explanations; they present a simple and direct explanation on all strategies – one at a time. It's free and one of the best sources in the world for learning all levels of option trading strategies. Keep this link handy, it is often much easier to find basic terms and quick information with this source, than it is to try and find it among the online trading platform instructions. Your trading platform training is geared to how to use your knowledge to trade and to learn great techniques. OIC, I think, should be your go-to for looking up terms and information on strategies quickly.

Many people who trade equity options already have their own sources and methods for stock selection. If you are a beginner, you'll need a basic understanding of the terms and markets as well as understanding fundamental and technical analysis. Although there are investors who use fundamental or technical analysis; the majority of investors use a combination of both. An experienced and flexible option trader is looking for timing and price predictability whether the underlying bias might be bearish, neutral, or bullish – there is always an option strategy to fit the market bias.

8 Options for Income

There are two kinds of people in the casino: the people who own them and the people who lose money in them. About 80% of all options expire worthless. Would you rather buy them or sell them? If there is any secret about options, if there is any strategy the professionals and veteran traders use - that you absolutely must know, this is it.

– the author

Selling Options

Selling options is also called writing options. Writing an option is like the written words you are reading right now; until someone wrote them, they didn't exist. Writing options used to be a lot riskier than it is now; the math is still the same but the information about these trades is light years ahead of where it was just ten years ago. Imagine comparing the accuracy of a long range cannon in 1945 - with the razor sharp accuracy of modern laser-guide missiles, and you will understand the efficacy of modern online option trading using powerful computers and cutting-edge software. The option analytics of even 10 years ago is child's play compared with the information and trading power available to the average trader now. The playing field between professionals and individual investors has been leveled.

Not everyone who decides to step-up their option trading will succeed. The people dazzled by the opportunity to make a quick fortune with little work and only short, quick study will be disappointed. Trading options successfully is a learned skill that experience sharpens. If you do your homework, it is quite possible to begin to make money right away; you have the opportunity to turn your intellectual efforts and self-discipline into money – and trading options online for many of us - is a fun and exciting way to do it. Two common characteristics, *complexity* and the sometimes (theoretical) *unlimited risk* will prevent most people from doing it.

Your cellphone has more processing power in it than Apollo 11 - the first manned mission landing on the moon. Don't think for a moment that option trading or learning to trade is anything like it was even ten years ago.

You certainly should not make the mistake of letting anyone tell you that learning to trade options successfully can't be done without years of study or that you need to buy expensive software. The old concept that only seasoned, veteran, professionals, with years of study behind them are worthy of advanced trading is dying rapidly; the world has changed. While it is true that many smart and creative people have paved the way for us – and we are grateful - it is also true that *times have changed and we must adapt.* A person can chat over live video while their car backs itself into a parallel parking place, so there is absolutely no reason individual investors can't use the similar forward technology to learn to trade options successfully.

In January 2002, one of my articles on option trading appeared in STOCKS & COMMODITIES MAGAZINE. It is titled *Ride The Tide Of Volatility - The Third Dimension Of Option Trading.* I thought having a few articles published would look good on my resume, so I spent two or three days writing the article and if memory serves, they paid only a couple of hundred dollars for the article. What is remarkable is - at the time- I was using an advanced option modeling program that cost over $3,000, paying almost another thousand dollars a month for data (quotes and software volatility data), and I had spent several years learning to use it all expertly. *That was then.* Now, you can get more information, more live free data, better software, and more than 100 times the computing power – all FREE in the comfort of your home or office. I also learned that writing magazine articles didn't even come close to paying what trading options paid!

There will always be a place for option gurus, the true master traders who can teach, and full-service brokers that make a living helping clients find and execute viable trades. The commissions for these types of brokers are generally ten times the deep discount online trading charges. You might turn out to be a trader who prefers trading by discussing risks, strategy, and trade selection with an industry professional, or you might be a person who can do it all on their own. Having contact and exchanging ideas with professionals and/or other traders that can help you –and can be a valuable avenue. I constantly read blogs, books, try new software, and I enjoy hearing about other people's ideas and trading experiences. But when it comes to trading, I get away from all the noise- and prefer the solitude of my own keyboard or touch-screen. After all, no matter how much I read and talk, I am the only person who will take full responsibility and consequences of the trades I place. Put another way, nobody who ever gave me an investment tip offered to pay my losses if their tip turned out to be wrong. Any advertised 'money back guarantee' – no matter how wonderful it may sound - will never include your trading losses. Remember that.

Selling Options: What Can Go Wrong

If you have opened an account to trade options using advanced strategies, then you may have noticed you were supplied (by law) a lot of fine print to read that warns you that such trading can involve high risk and large losses. It's true, and you should never forget it. Coupled with the inherent risks of these trades, the very human predilection of almost reflexively and instinctively wanting to hold trades that go bad long enough for them to turn around and improve – is a deadly combination.

It sounds so easy to sell an OTM option with a 90% chance of expiring OTM. You can make money very often with such a strategy but when it goes wrong, it can get ugly in a hurry – and you should never forget it. Since risk and reward are commensurate, selling far OTM options will give you a high chance of success but the trade off is that you won't get to collect large premiums for taking these smaller risks. Consequently, when just one of these trades backfires, it can wipe out the profits of many successful trades. If you are a beginner, use the discipline to only sell options on a very limited basis until you go through the experience of managing some losers. When you trade, always have an exit plan for all contingencies. There is a balance to option trading, if you are too careful or not careful enough – either of these, figuratively speaking of course, can get you (your account) killed.

The classic beginner's mistake is to be successful four or five times in a row and get overconfident and drop your caution; this is when you can lose it all. Selling naked (uncovered) options can be extremely risky. Once every few years, debacles happen that you won't see coming – and when it happens and you have the large risk exposure, it can wipe out months and years of successful investing.

Ok, the warnings have been issued, so now I can tell you the good news: Using option spreads can allow you to sell options while simultaneously limiting (insurance) your losses. You might not make as much on each trade, but that is merely the tradeoff for limiting the risk. There is no free lunch, but you knew that, right? Learning to use option spread trades allows you to limit your risk exposure. There are plenty more income opportunities in the spread trading sections of this book.

There Are No Non-Professional Traders

pro·fes·sion·al
/prəˈfeSH(ə)n(ə)l/

noun -

(of a person) engaged in an occupation as a paid job rather than as a hobby

In my world, there is no such thing as hobby money unless you count bogus money of a board game. One exception might be the activity of buying lotto tickets. Lotto tickets, as someone pointed out, are little more than *a tax on people who are bad at math.*

Casinos biggest money-maker of all the games they offer – is the slot machine and yet most slots payout more than 97% of the money put into them by customers. The locals in Las Vegas know where to find the highest payouts and therefore the best odds; many commonly have payouts near 98% and still, they make more money for the casino than any other games. The reason slot machines make the most money is because they are easy to use, not intimidating, and a customer can even be drunk and the impairment won't change the odds significantly. Slot machines are pretty much brainless fun; this is why they are popular and also why they are the biggest money-makers for the casinos – not by a little bit but by far the most profitable. I'm all for having brainless fun, just not when I'm investing my money.

Since about 80% of options expire worthless, the general odds are 4/5th's in your favor. If you don't know how to choose your strategies and manage your trades, even these odds are not enough to make you consistent money. If you doubt this, remember that slot machines commonly payout more than 97% of the money put into them and yet a vast majority of people who play them lose. If it entertains them, some people don't mind losing at all, so they keep losing over and over again. In trading options, you have a chance to select strategies, risk amounts, and the odds.

Learning to sell options is a professional endeavor and once you learn it and gain experience – doing so can be a lifelong profit center and source of income. The wonderful thing about selling options is that when compared to opening most businesses, it is inexpensive and - if you are willing to put in the study and discipline- there can be a very high probability of success. Like owning a slot machine, you don't have any employees to manage, you make money even when you are sleeping or on vacation, and you can constantly have the law of numbers working for you as sure as gravity is consistent. Please note, I didn't say its easy; I said it's possible.

One of the common mistakes people make when learning to trade options is to make a risky trade with the feeling that you are out-smarting the market. Within this mistake is another common mistake: thinking that one of your first trades *won't cost you a lot even if you lose* and that – win or lose – is a costly habit. This is what I call 'lotto thinking'. If you lose your money a dollar at a time, the losses almost always seem tolerable; this is slot-machine thinking – and blind luck will not often pay very well in games like lotto or slots where the odds are very intentionally (and fairly stated to you) against you. Nobody makes you play slots or lotto; it's a choice.

I was at a convenience store one evening and there was a long line at the checkout, so I engaged in chitchat with a couple of people in line behind me that were waiting to buy weekly lotto tickets. I repeated the joke that 'lotto is a tax on people who are bad at math' and they didn't laugh or even smile; they were serious. They did tell me what everyone knows – that the odds are slim but the payout can be life-changing. I made them an offer only an options seller would think of. I offered, "If you will pay me one dollar, I will give you 10 chances at making $1,000. You pick 10 sets of lotto numbers with a Powerball kicker, and if any of them win – I will pay you a thousand dollars. I'll put it in writing and even let someone hold the money so you can be sure to get paid if you win." Of course, they refused because they knew I would win, and yet they stood in line with money in their hand so they could willfully take on odds 1000's of times greater than what I offered them. (Odds of winning a recent Powerball drawing were one in 175 million, and one in 5.15 million of winning the second prize of one million dollars.) The dream of putting up a small amounts of money to get a big payoff is as attractive to humans in the same way a bright light is to bugs. In order to have a much better chance of winning money, they had to give up what they really expected: the feeling that they had a possibility of becoming enormously wealthy with little or no effort. For paying their dollar per chance, they get to feel that way for up to a week, and if they chose better odds by taking me up on my offer, they would never feel so good because they know a thousand dollars will never change their lifestyle. And that is the fantasy, that keeps them coming back, often for a lifetime.

The reason I tell this story at all is that traders (I think) must know that deep inside themselves, far under the surface, that they have at least some inclination towards 'lotto' thinking. We humans didn't evolve to the top of the food chain by not taking some risks; it's in our DNA. If you feel the urge (and you probably will at some time), then go buy a lotto ticket and get it out of your system; just don't let that sort of thinking invade your investment account – at least not the options trading portion of your investments. Just one of these 'fun larks' can destroy your investment earnings.

Doing the math: Why would a Las Vegas local go to where the payout on slot machine is 98% instead of 97%? This doesn't sound like much difference. The math: Slots with 98% instead of 97% pay out 50% more to winners, while keeping only 1% less of the total money put into them. The casino makes less per customer but has more customers. This is common knowledge among regular local players in casino cities like Las Vegas; while the casino still profits 2% of all the money run through their slots. State scratch-off tickets don't pay out even 50%, but they can still put pictures of slot machines on the tickets!

Volume and Open Interest
Vol & OI

Open interest: The total number of outstanding option contracts on a given series or for a given underlying stock. **Volume:** The number of trades (usually for the day)

		Symbol	Price		
Stock:	Wal-mart	**WMT**	**81.20**		
CALLS	Class	Days until Exp			
	MAY 15	39			
Strike:	**Bid**	**Ask**	**O.I.**	**Volume**	**Prob OTM**
75	5.65	6.50	45	2	0.00%
77.5	3.95	4.20	341	0	22.20%
80	2.19	2.26	699	139	41.46%
82.5	0.96	0.98	2,454	85	65.37%
85	0.35	0.38	35,078	579	83.96%
87.5	0.09	0.13	5,607	3	94.21%

This example using WMT is here to illustrate the OI and Vol of an option class. The underlying is trading at 81.20. The WMT MAY 85 CALL is trading bid/ask .35/.38. It has 35,078 open contracts, and 579 have traded on the day. The Prob of OTM at expiration - is 83.96%. Let's assume you could sell five of them for .36, the credit would be $36 x 5 = $180 less commissions. At commissions of $10 per option, the credit would be $130. At $1.50 per option, the credit would be $172.50. Since the bid/ask gap is fairly *narrow* at .35/.38, the OI is *high* at 35,078, and the volume is not scant at 579 – it should be no problem to expect to sell five of the options near our target of .36 each. On the other hand, had we found few OI, very low volume, and a wider bid/ask gap – this trade even though listed, might not be feasible.

One parameter (not shown in this table) sometimes used - is the *theoretical value* of an option. The displayed bid/ask prices on high OI and good volume will normally be fairly accurate, but if the gap is very wide (for example had it been .30/.42, you probably need to know a theoretical value to get a better idea of what the option should be worth. Your trading platform software allows you to select from any/all of the option parameters at any time for your display. You can change the parameters on your matrix display easily, usually by drop down menu at the column headings. Since the matrix has limits to its number of headings displayed at once (width space restrictions depending on the font size and your software), it is not possible to display all the parameters at once, nor is it really necessary – as it would have the effect of cluttering your screen with information you neither need or use on a regular basis. Just to review: A reminder that *thinly traded* strikes might have a wide bid/ask gap and not reflect efficient (fair) option prices. The ideal is to have high OI and high volume, but when you are trading far OTM options, you can't always find this ideal – so you need to pay close attention that you don't sell options too cheaply. Remember, the price you get is an important factor in your ROI (return on investment), even though the option may have a satisfactory Prob of OTM, High OI, and Vol, you need to know if you must exit a trade quickly, that there will be enough activity (volume) to do so at a fair (efficient) price.

This particular example: Sell five of the WMT MAY 85 CALLS @ .36 ($36) has to reflect some confidence of your opinion of the price movement of the underlying. Ignoring commissions, the break even price of WMT at expiration in 39 days = strike price + option premium = 85 + .36 = 85.36. The worst-case scenario is the underlying goes up to infinity, you could have infinite losses. If the stock was 86.36 at expiration, you would lose a net of $1.00 per share or 500 shares x $1.00 = -$500.

How sensitive is your trade to fluctuations in the price of WMT shares? The delta of the short option (not shown in table) is .17. This means (all things remaining the same) a $1.00 change in the underlying price would cause a .17 ($17 change) in the option's price.

Don't get so involved in the option trade that you are distracted from your analysis of the underlying's price movement. If you are trading a stock price that correlates strongly with the S&P Index, NASDAQ Index, or the DJIA, then you realize that factors other than the fundamentals of a stock will influence its price. Every year after the Christmas holiday season, the nation's largest retailer announces how its sales faired; the stock price of WMT is subject to surprises, so this time period might be a riskier than usual to sell the CALLS. On the other hand, if you made this trade at a time when the economy in general was fairing poorly, WMT would probably not be subject to huge gains in sales (and stock price). Most certainly, you should be aware of expected earnings and dates the reports are released. In this case, there are only 39 days until expiration – so the trade could be timed literally, between earnings reports to avoid these sorts of surprises. The more you know and learn about the underlying's price behavior, the more creative you may be when placing your trades.

Certain stocks and groups of stocks may be regularly influenced by things such as currency exchange rates (particularly if their earnings are derived from exports/overseas sales for example). Most bank stocks are sensitive to changes in interest rates, as would be loan companies, insurance companies, and others.

Beware of headlines: This morning I heard an automobile manufacturer had "....larger than expected gains in the latest earnings report." A close look at the details revealed they made (minus) -$1.26 for the quarter instead of the expected (minus) -$1.32. This same sort of thing is sometimes called a 'turnaround' and even those words suggest marked improvement, the difference in reality is hardly significant at all. Never mind the headlines, get the facts.

One sure way to avoid most stock price surprises is to build a stable of your favorites and follow them religiously. By keeping a list on your daily quote screen you use most often, you will constantly be exposed to their prices, you can monitor news items, earnings reports, dividend payments, and dozens of other factors that influence its pricing. Even more importantly, you will – just by seeing them everyday – build a library of the stock's price fluctuations in your head. The more you 'stalk' a stock, the more comfortable you will be in predicting its behavior. I cannot overstate the value of doing this; over time, you will develop this list into your 'go to' stocks. If you build a list and discover that half the list are dull and uninteresting to your liking, then change it. The more you enjoy this following of certain stocks (or other products like ETF, Index, currency, commodities, etc.), the better you will naturally maintain your interest in learning about them. Enthusiasm is power; use it wisely.

If you happen to have an expertise in banking, solar power, automobile sales, chemistry, computers, gaming, or any other area that you can translate to a stock you will like to follow

– then go for it. Even if its something you don't yet know, over time that learning and attention to it - can pay off and pay well.

I once taught a beginners course at a local college on commodity investing, a summertime non-credit course. I limited the class to a dozen people as I wanted to keep it intimate and get the chance to learn about the participants and to be able to answer their questions individually. The class met once a week for twelve weeks. The first few sessions were to cover the basics, the terms and methods that are commonly used in selecting markets to trade. My advice is always to suggest that people trade 'what they know' if possible. About half way through the course, about eight of the dozen students had opened accounts and begun trading. This was the fun part of the course; each week students would either bring in the results of actual trades or paper trades and we would study each one. This is a great way to learn and with the small class we were all rooting for each other, not trying to impress anyone but just enjoying the advantages of honest exchanges.

It soon became apparent that only one person in the class had consistent and remarkable success. He was one of only three of the dozen that were already trading with real money instead of paper money. He was in his 70's, the oldest member of the class; he only volunteered information when he was asked. His name was Carl and he had been trading Natural Gas futures with great success. In his first four trades, and he brought his statements to class, he made over $12,500. Had we not asked him directly, I don't think he would have ever mentioned his unusual success; he had a matter-of-fact demeanor and was not the least bit eager to brag or impress anyone. This, of course, only made us all like him and appreciate his comments even more.

Carl explained to us the reason he had traded Natural Gas and nothing else is because he 'knew nothing' about commodities. He told us his son worked out of Louisiana and worked on a Natural Gas rig out in the Gulf of Mexico. He said every time a hurricane threat was nearing the Gulf, his son would phone ahead and let him know he was going to use the time off to come home for a few days. The natural gas businesses that own rigs out in the oceans have the most advanced weather modeling in the world; they have to because they have billions of dollars of equipment and the safety of their workers to protect. Carl explained his strategy in only a few words, "Every time my son phoned to say he was coming, I would BUY, then when he got the advanced notice to go back to work, I'd SELL. And that's how I traded my money. I traded four times and only lost a little money once." Carl's common sense and ability to recognize that good ideas can be incredibly simple were the reason for his success.

I love to tell this story because it always reminds me of how often we outsmart ourselves and fail to see the simple opportunities that are in our own backyard, directly under our noses. Over the years, I discovered that a great many people know things that one can turn into investment opportunities. With options, since you can make money no matter which way or how far a market moves – the opportunities are much greater than just trying to buy a stock and guess the direction its price is headed. For example, just being confident that a stock's price might trade within a wide range for the next 30 to 60 days is enough to place a trade with an over 90% probability of success. It is precisely for this reason that I say option trading is much easier than stock or commodity trading alone.

9 BUYING CALLS

When you buy a CALL, you own the *right* to *buy* 100 shares of the underlying at the STRIKE price during a fixed period of time, until its expiration date. If you want to take a little money and have the opportunity to leverage it - and make more, then this is a strategy to consider.

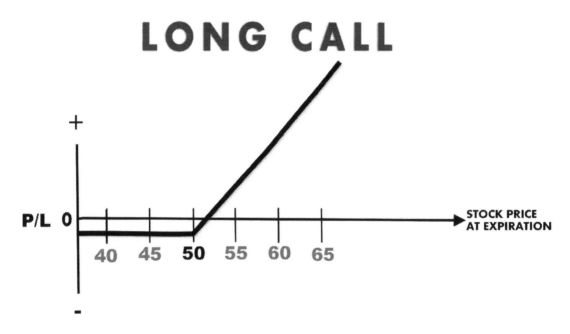

LONG CALL

EXAMPLE:

BUY 1 XYZ 50 CALL

MARKET VIEW: BULLISH
IV%: lower, moving up

MAXIMUM GAIN: Unlimited
MAXIMUM LOSS: Price of CALL
BREAK-EVEN: Strike + Option Price

(the prices and options used here are for illustration only and all the number will have changed by publication date of course).

Example: BUY AAPL OCT 125 CALL @ 10.77

The price of one CALL is $1077. This purchase gives the buyer the right (not obligation) to buy 100 shares of the underlying AAPL at a price of $125/share. The maximum risk is the price of the option. Buying the shares instead would cost $12,763, and the theoretical loss the same - if the stock goes to zero. Of course AAPL is not going to zero – so the risk is much less. Buying the option instead of the stock, the worst case is to lose the premium of $1077; the AAPL OCT 125 CALL will expire worthless, if the underlying is not above 125 at expiration.

The break-even on the trade at expiration is the strike price plus the premium paid = AAPL would need to be 125 + 10.77 = $135.77. There are 15,055 of this 125 strike trading, and during the day in progress 37 of these CALLS have traded.

The delta of the AAPL OCT 125 CALL is presently .57; this means the option might increase or decrease by .57 for each change in AAPL price of $1.00.

		Symbol	Price	
Stock:	Apple	AAPL	127.63	
CALLS	Class	Days until Exp		
	OCT 15	192		
Strike:	Price	Delta	Volume	OI
105	24.40	0.84	0	6,037
110	20.40	0.79	0	5,956
115	16.80	0.72	126	18,155
120	13.60	0.65	143	23,076
125	10.77	0.57	37	15,055
130	8.43	0.49	746	27,205
135	6.45	0.41	33	17,674
140	4.88	0.33	13	10,709
145	3.63	0.27	7	7,400
150	2.69	0.21	26	57,773

This is a good time to have you examine option price behavior: Notice AAPL is trading at 127.63 in this example. The nearest CALL strike in-the-money (ITM) is the 125 strike and its delta is .57. As a rule of thumb ATM (at-the-money) options should have a delta of about .50. The 125 is slightly in-the-money so its delta is just a little over .50 at .57. The 130 strike CALL is just OTM and has a delta slightly less than .50 at .49. The far-out-of-the-money 150 CALL has a delta of only .21. If AAPL went up $5.00 per share, the 150 strike will gain about 5.00 x .21 = 1.05 in value from the present 2.69 to 3.74, an increase of 39% in value on the five dollar price move of the underlying stock.

Let's compare that to the slightly in-the-money 125 CALL with a delta of .57: AAPL goes up $5.00 per share, so the option we bought at 10.77 goes to [10.77 +(5.00 x .57)] = 13.62, or a gain of 26.5%. If AAPL's five dollar move was down instead of up, the absolute change in value would be about the same – and the trade would be in the red instead of black.

Now, let's compare these gains with an outright buy of 100 of AAPL @ 127.63 = $12,763. A five dollar price move would be equal to $500 ($5 x 100 shares). $500 is exactly 3.9% of the purchase price. Plus, you would have the risk of the option price ONLY with the CALL trade, but the potential (not necessarily the probable) loss of the entire stock value.

When you buy a CALL or PUT option, the most you ever are at risk is its price. Another fact you can glean from the AAPL CALL matrix, is that daily volume of individual CALL strikes is less, the further OTM the strike price is; this is a typical pattern.

Go back to our original trade example: We bought the AAPL OCT 125 CALL @ 10.77: Let's look at various outcomes and the choices of the buyer of this CALL. Note that the CALL bought has an intrinsic value (ITM value) of 2.63 (127.63 minus the strike of 125); the remainder of the premium is *extrinsic* value, the time value and value due to implied volatility (IV%).

Managing the Long CALL position:

You have choices. Most investors who buy CALLS do not hold them until expiration, nor do they (if they are ITM) exercise their right to buy the underlying at the strike price. Most investors will sell the CALL prior to the expiration date.

If the value of the CALL has decreased sufficiently, the owner may choose to sell the CALL and take a loss. At any time prior to expiration , the owner of the CALL may sell it. If the underlying price advances and the investor wished to liquidate (make a closing sale) the long CALL, they may sell it for a profit if its value is higher than when they purchased it.

In the example of buying the AAPL 125 strike CALL for 10.77: The owner of the CALL may, at any time prior to expiration exercise the CALL and buy the underlying stock at the strike price. The full cost-basis of the stock would be the strike price + the premium paid for the option, which would be 125 + 10.77 = 136.77 in this case. Unless the CALL is ITM, of course it makes no sense to exercise it.

Most option traders would cut losses and sell the CALL if the trade isn't working. Few option traders hold the option until expiration; they may take a profit on the option at any time they choose. This raises a good question: When should a trader take the profits? The answer is: There is no 'should point', you must make your own rules, depending on many factors including but not limited to: your opinion of price movement of the underlying in the time left until expiration, the theta (time-decay), target price points that satisfy your goal on the trade, your aversion to risk, your money management plan, and sometimes your ability to closely monitor the trade. Some traders will put in a limit sell order GTC (good till cancelled), if they can't monitor the trade closely or choose not to do so.

Personally, when I have a 36% gain on the trade in a few days, I just shout 'Thank You' and take the money. I do know traders that commonly use a 25% or 50% point on their positions as a trigger to exit the trade and move on. Unlike straight stock trading, the option has a finite life. In this way they are like the expiration date on milk and something must be done with them.; they are not totally passive investments. There is yet another choice, you could sell the CALL and buy another higher strike, if and only if you are very bullish. As the old saying goes, "You can go to the well too often and it could be dry." *Rolling out* is a practice mostly done when shorting/selling options; we'll discuss this in more detail soon.

There are very long-term (over 12 months) options. This definition is from the OCC, Options Clearing Corporation and the OIC, Options Industry Council:

There are Long-Term Equity AnticiPation Securities® (LEAPS®). If you want to get the same effect of a long term buy and hold position; these options LEAPS® offer investors an alternative to stock ownership. LEAPS® calls enable investors to benefit from stock price rises while risking less capital than required to purchase stock. If a stock price rises to a level above the exercise price of the LEAPS®, the buyer may exercise the option and purchase shares at a price below the current market price. The same investor may sell the LEAPS® calls in the open market for a profit.

Many stocks also have *weekly* options; you will see these classes on your trading software right along with the monthly classes. There are traders that specialize in these very short term options. I won't discount their usefulness or opportunity, but normally I would advise beginner and intermediate level traders to learn the basics (stay with the monthly classes) before trading them.

Here's a review for you, a few Q&A's on options:

How often does the buyer of an option exercise it?
Normally, the buyer of a CALL just wants to make a profit, not to own the stock. It is quite normal and the routine to exit the trade prior to expiration. The investor purchases an option contract but will be out of the trade before the contact ends and he or she never intends to exercise the option(s).

When are my options automatically exercised?
Short answer: If they are in-the-money at expiration, they *will* be exercised. To avoid this, exit the trade. They may be exercised at any time (American style options).

How important is it to check the OI and volume of an option before trading it?
If you are trading options on a well-known and active stock, checking the OI and volume can give you some insight as to what other trader's interest is. If you are new to option trading, you may not yet have the experience to know that some thinly traded stocks have even more

thinly (less frequently) traded options. Checking the real time bid/ask in any trade is a must; if those bid/ask gaps are wide, just putting in a market order is never a good idea. Until you gain some experience, you are better off not taking a lark on options that are thinly traded with low open interest – these are the flags of skewed option values since there is not enough OI and volume to present an efficient (fairly priced values) market.

What is the deadline on option expiration day?
Usually, shortly after 4PM ET on the Friday expiration date. Not a good idea to cut it too close, if its going to cost you money. By the way, an option that is out-of-the-money will not be *automatically* exercised. If you sold an option and it is expiring OTM (worthless) for sure, you are not required to do anything; the premium has already been credited to your account and it stays there automatically.

When do I need to use a market order when purchasing or selling options?
If you are buying the option, a market order will fill at the ask-price. Conversely, if you are selling an option a market order will fill at the bid-price. Most traders use limit orders to fix the trade price, but using a market order when there is no wide gap in the bid/ask and volume is fast is just fine. It is quite common to see a gap of .05 in the bid/ask. Sometimes checking the theoretical price can give you an estimation of where the option price should be. Just like when you are trading stocks, there is depth to the bid/ask both above and below the current price.

Why do I need to look at the IV% of options before trading them?
Using the IV% parameter can give you some idea of the value of trading a specific option. Generally speaking the higher the IV% the more value the market places on the time value and the volatility of the underlying. IV% values are comprised solely of time-value and the likelihood of the option gaining or losing value. If you are buying an option, check the IV% of nearby strikes in the same class; when compared to nearby options, if the IV% is relatively high – this indicates the market values the option more. It is normal for IV% values to be higher as the strikes of PUTS and CALLS get farther OTM. Keep in mind, IV% is a comparative measure; normally, you compare IV% in the same class of the same stock's options. Comparing the IV% of one stock's against the IV% of another stock's options is not normally done as it isn't useful. As you gain experience trading, your eye will become trained to common patterns of IV%. There are traders who actually 'trade volatility'; their goal is to

make money on increases and decreases of volatility – and perhaps less on the direction of the price movement. The goal is to have both the IV% and price trends in favor of your trade. Trading solely on volatility is definitely a very advanced technique for experienced option traders. When examining an option class matrix (for example: the XYZ SEP CALLS/PUTS), all other things being the same, the options with the highest IV% are commonly said to be *more expensive;* their value is directly proportional to the implied volatility.

Which class (days until expiration) of option should I use?

You may as well ask which tool in my toolbox do I choose? The answer of course, depends on the job to be done. If you are buying a CALL to gain rise in the underlying, the options time-decay works against you, so it probably isn't wise to use an options with a life of under 45 to 30 days. Go back and look at the graph on time decay (page 47) and you will see the decay of time value increases very fast as the option nears the last 30 days of an option's life. Since this is the same thing that could make buying a CALL cheap, a beginner might not yet understand that an option farther out in time (that cost more) would be a better play because its time-value decay is much slower. Conversely, if you are *selling* a single option strike (not a combo trade), selling an option with less than 45 to 30 days until expiration is desirable, and a good tactic to use. Remember that theta is the amount an option should decrease in value per trading day.

Which strike price should I use?

The answer to this type question depends on many factors. Here's a simple example if you are buying a CALL because you expect to make a profit as the underlying increases in price. Let's say XYZ is trading at $32.50 per share, and the 35-strike about six months out - has a delta of .25 and is bid/ask at 1.20/1.50. You do a quick check and find the *theoretical value* (Theo Price) of the option is 1.35. You check the OI/volume and the IV% and compare it to the other options in the matrix in this class – and you feel that paying 1.35 would be a fair price. With a delta of .25, you see the option would likely increase in value by $25 for each 1.00 rise in the underlying XYZ share price. Now, another parameter of this trade becomes important when choosing a strike: How much do you expect the impending (time scope) price move to be in magnitude? If the answer is- you expect about a 4.00 move up from 32.50 to the area of $36 to $40, then –with a *delta* of .25, you might expect your option to increase in value on a 4.00 move of (.25 x 4) about $100 per option. If you are buying the option to get leverage on your investment dollar, consider that buying 100 shares of the stock outright would cost you $3,250. The good news is that option only cost $135 (1.35), and you could get a profit of $100, a 75% profit. Since the option's *delta* is .25, you can buy four of them (4 x $135) for $540 and the combined **delta** (the delta of the trade) is about 1.0, which means buying four of them will give you the same (potential) gains as owning 100 shares. You have learned that an at-the-money option will have a *delta* of about .50, so you could buy two at-the-money CALLS and get about the same result; you might price both strategies and decide which you like the best. I placed this example here because you should learn not only what the term *delta* means, but how to begin to use it to evaluate your trades, not just to project what your profits might be. Algebraically add the individual deltas to get the **net delta** of your trade. Remember CALLS have a positive delta, and PUTS a negative delta.

What if I bought a CALL and have profits in the trade, but since it is still a long time until the options expires, I fear my profit could disappear?

Whether you simply trade stocks on the short term or use options, this is a quite common dilemma – and a good dilemma because you have profits! The simple answer is 'take the money; there's bulls, bears, and pigs.' But let's make this question more difficult by assuming that you think the stock has a ways to go up yet. If you are long the CALL option(s) instead of the stock, you have other choices available. You can do a combination trade that is commonly called a vertical bull spread. When you own a CALL and want to lock-in at least some of the profit without exiting the trade completely, you simply keep the CALL and sell a higher strike CALL. In the example just used, you bought four of the XYZ 35 strike CALLS for 1.35 and the trade has a net delta of 1.0; let's suppose the underlying advances six dollars a share and your gains are $600. Now, with XYZ trading at (32.50 + 6.00) 38.50, the 40-strike option is now trading at 1.90. Sell four of the XYZ 40-strike @ 1.90 and get the credit of (4 x $190) $760 in your account. Having added this leg to the trade, you turned the CALL into a *vertical bull spread* at a credit (net profit on your position) of $760 minus your cost in buying the four 35-strike CALLS (4 x $135= $540). Your net credit is $760 minus $540 = $220. Now, you get to keep the $220, no matter what -- and if the underlying prices rises to $40 or above, you make the 5.00 gain on each of the four spreads or a total additional potential profit of (4 x $500) $2000. The net result is that you have chosen to risk $380 of your $600 profit, in exchange for a potential profit of up to $2,000. It is fun to think of this as pocketing $220 and then having a *free* trade left. It wasn't free at all of course, it cost you $380 of *sure money* to make this conversion. Your net break-even stock- price-at-expiration on the four vertical bull spreads you have left would be [(3.8/4)+ 35] = 35.95 price for XYZ at expiration. So you could make additional money over the $220 credit you pocketed. If at expiration the price of XYZ was 35.95 or greater on the equivalent of 400 shares up to a price of 40 per share.

VERTICAL BULL SPREAD

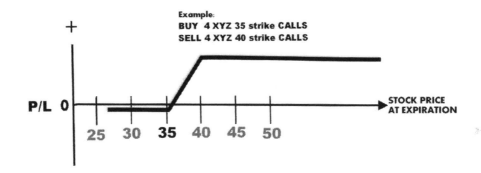

Example:
BUY 4 XYZ 35 strike CALLS
SELL 4 XYZ 40 strike CALLS

MARKET VIEW: Bullish

MAXIMUM GAIN: Upper Strike minus lower strike - net premium paid

MAXIMUM LOSS: Net Premium Paid

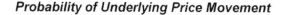

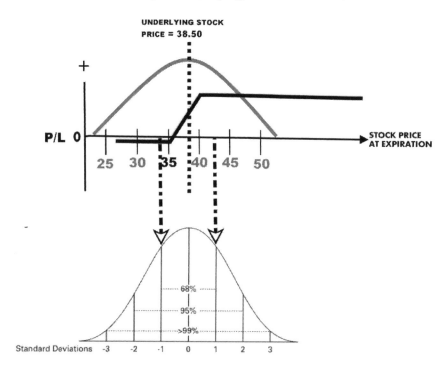

How Understanding Probability Can Reduce Trade Cost

Let's analyze the Vertical Bull (CALL) Spread in the last example: We are long XYZ 35 STRIKE CALLS and short (sold) the XYZ 40 STRIKE CALLS. This will show you how to reduce the effective cost of a bullish option trade by understanding the statistical distribution of probability. With the underlying XYZ at 38.50 at the time we place the vertical bull spread, we can easily see how much more likely it is that the price of XYZ will be within one SD (standard deviation 68%) at options expiration. Since we have nothing to gain if the stock is under 33 or over 43, why pay to trade those ranges when we don't have to? Simply put, by not paying to trade ranges that are not nearly as likely or profitable, we can reduce the cost of the trade by selling the 40 call for a *credit*. The stock price only has a 32% chance of trading outside of the first standard deviation (68%). ***This type of trade is what makes Vertical Bull Spreads a favorite of option traders; it has the effect of focusing your money where the highest chance of reward is.*** Be sure you understand this section, even if you have to go to other sources and find more examples of the Vertical Bull Spread. Your brain's 'light bulb' should go "on" here; this is the crux in understanding how to fashion option trades to get the most bang for your buck. You pay less and only trade the price range that has a higher probability of profit; this is a more efficient way of trading. In later sections of this book, we'll show you how to use what are called *ratio spreads* and how to use *vertical bear spreads* - and for advanced traders, the use of *strangles* and *straddles* to trade price and/ or volatility.

It is commonly understood how using options can *leverage* your money. The shaping of trades to have the highest chance of profiting per dollar invested is not something as widely understood; for years only professional traders had the information and software to use these advantages. Now, online trading platforms have brought this knowledge into the realm of everyday individual investors. I've coined the term *Options Exposed* to describe this gateway to modern option trading. It means to bring the process of learning advanced option trading to individual investors that use online trading platforms and super-low commissions.

The most revolutionary thing about modern individual investors trading options - is that the same software and computers that makes it possible to use these advanced strategies, also empowers anyone to learn option trading faster and easier than ever before possible.

10 BUYING PUTS

When you buy a PUT, you own the *right* to *sell* 100 shares of the underlying at the STRIKE price during a fixed period of time, until its expiration date. This strategy, the risks, and trading methods are pretty much identical to buying a CALL, except you hold a negative market view (bearish).

If you own a stock and portend a price decline, one choice you have is to sell the stock. Another choice is to buy a PUT; as the price of the underlying goes down, the PUT increases in value. Profits of the long PUT may partially or fully offset losses you incur by being long (owning) the underlying stock- when they are used to hedge.

LONG PUT

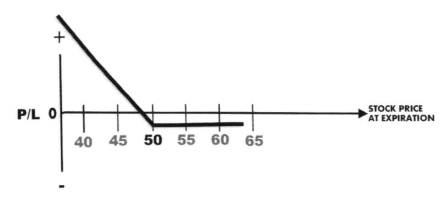

EXAMPLE:

BUY 1 XYZ 50 PUT

MARKET VIEW: BEARISH
IV%: lower & moving up

MAXIMUM GAIN: Strike Price - Option Price
MAXIMUM LOSS: Price of PUT
BREAK-EVEN: Strike less Option Price

Example: You own 100 shares of General Electric. The current price is 25.01. Scenario: You bought the stock at a much lower price a year ago, and now you suspect there could be a price decline over the next few weeks and you want to protect your profits by buying a PUT.

Of course, buying the PUT doesn't keep the price of the stock from declining but the increase in the value of the PUT will offset the stock's price decline (a *hedge*), if any – between now and the expiration date of the PUT(S). Look at the PUT matrix: The options will expire in 99 days; let's assume you have determined that term (timing) is suitable.

		Symbol	Price			
Stock:	General Elec	GE	25.01			
PUTS	Class	Days until Exp				
	JUL 15	99				
Strike:	Bid	Ask	Theo Price	Delta	OI	IV%
22	0.18	0.20	0.19	-0.13	230	24.77%
23	0.31	0.33	0.32	-0.21	457	20.98%
24	0.55	0.57	0.56	-0.34	1,326	17.74%
25	0.94	0.96	0.95	-0.52	7,926	15.01%
26	1.54	1.58	1.56	-0.71	858	11.66%
27	2.28	2.48	2.38	-0.84	81	3.00%
28	3.15	3.40	3.28	-0.93	51	4.00%
29	4.15	4.40	4.28	-0.93	0	0.00%

Take a moment to study the OI, and compare the theoretical price of each strike with the bid/ask. Notice the strikes with nearest to the money have the most efficient pricing (fair value) and also the highest open interest (OI) – and notice how the IV% (implied volatility) goes up as the PUTS are farther OTM. All these patterns are normal. Also notice how the delta of various strikes increases, the deeper ITM the strikes are. Again, this is the normal pattern. As you gain experience, that wonderful brain you have - will learn to scan for these patterns almost automatically; for now, practice recognizing these things. You will be amazed at how easy and natural it seems to be aware of these things, once you practice more.

Now, back to our example: You want to hedge a possible price drop in GE, so you can protect your profits. The 25 strike is at-the-money (stock price is 25.01); as expected the ATM delta of that strike is near -.50 at -.52 (remember the delta of PUTS are expressed as a negative number because the price change of the underlying will be *down*. Conversely, delta on all CALL options is a positive number.

Will simply buying one of the 25-strike puts give me 100% price protection from decreasing GE prices?
No; the delta is .52; if the price goes down by 3.50 per share the PUT should increase in value by (delta x price change) .52 x 3.50 x 100 shares = $182, while the stock value decreases 100 x 3.5 = $350. This only covers 52% of your losses due to the stock price decline. Buying two of these PUTS would give you a delta near -1.04.

What strike should I use to cover 100% of my potential losses of a price decline in GE?
Let's go 'option shopping': You could buy two of the 25-strikes for 104% (2 x delta of .52) protection; this cost would be two times .95 or 1.90 = $190. A one dollar price drop from 25.01 to 24.01 would yield an increase in the two PUT's value of -.52 delta x 2 PUTS x 1.0 [change in price] = $104 increase in the value of the two PUTS; that would offset the loss of $100 on 100 shares of stock. In reality, the delta would increase slightly as the 25-strike went in-the-money, so you'd probably have an increase near $122 instead of only $104. (How do I know this, the easy way? I can see in the matrix that the (theoretical) price of the 26-strike is 1.56 and *it is one dollar ITM*; thus I can assume the price of the 25-strike would probably move from 0.95 up to about 1.56, an increase of .61 (thus the two options would increase about (2 x .61) $122.

Another way to structure protection is to consider buying three of the 24-strikes for a combined delta near 1.0 (3 x -.34= -1.02). Or you could buy five of the 23-strike PUTS for a combined delta of near 1.0 (5 x -.21= -1.05). While the numbers are here in front of us, let me introduce you to a new term: *delta neutral*. The *delta* of long stock is 1.0, the delta of our PUT hedge (protection) is about -1.0. When you algebraically add the deltas of a trade's components, you get the *net delta*. In this case, +1 +(-1)= 0 or *delta zero*.

Your software trading platform will allow you to combine various strikes and types of options to place trades; one of the common parameters displayed for you, prior to you placing the trade, is the net delta of the *trade.* Your software computes it automatically - but you need to understand how it is derived so you can learn to use these numbers for quick reference to evaluate the efficacy of a particular trade. Knowing the delta of your trade also serves as a quick check to verify you are doing what you think you are doing - when you place the trade.

VERTICAL BEAR SPREAD

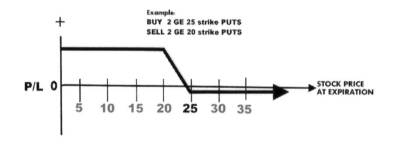

Example:
BUY 2 GE 25 strike PUTS
SELL 2 GE 20 strike PUTS

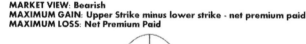

MARKET VIEW: Bearish
MAXIMUM GAIN: Upper Strike minus lower strike - net premium paid
MAXIMUM LOSS: Net Premium Paid

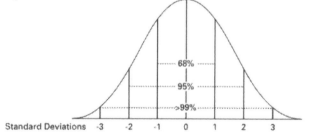

You can also use a Vertical Bear Spread: Buy PUTS and simultaneously sell PUTS of a lower strike. This still covers a high probability of price movement and it usually costs less. You can also, in our GE example buy two 25-strike PUTS and then IF the price goes down, *leg*

into the other side of the Vertical Bear Spread by selling them at a higher premium than is available now.

Legging into a combination trades is a term commonly used. Here's how the OIC, Options Industry Council defines a *leg*:

A term describing one side of a position with two or more sides. When a trader legs into a spread, they establish one side first, hoping for a favorable price movement in order to execute the other side at a better price. This is a higher-risk method of establishing a spread position.

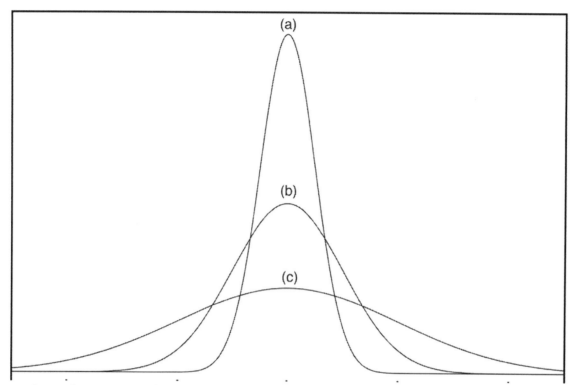

Nominal Distribution of Probability and a Stock's Price Movement

In price volatility illustration so far, I've only use the mathematically perfect random curve, commonly called the Bell curve. To have a proper understanding of how volatility modeling is performed on stock prices, we have to go a bit deeper. In this illustration- there are three nominal distribution curves representing relative levels of an underlying's volatility. (a) being the lowest, (b) mid-range, and (c) the highest volatility. The 'Value of X' or horizontal axis represents change in the (underlying) stock price. The % volatility is directly proportional to the likelihood of a price change in either direction. The lower the volatility, the higher or steeper the curve, indicating the stock's narrower expected trading range. Conversely, the higher the volatility, the flatter the curve is. All of these curves have symmetrical halves, that is –from the middle or peak – the curves trail off in either direction equally. Advanced veteran traders, some of them, are quick to point out that many of these curves in fact have asymmetric characteristics, and they would be quite correct. Your trading software platform, as mentioned previously, will compensate for the fact that stocks have an infinite upside and downside limited to a stock price of zero, if you use the *log normal* parameter on your displays. An investor who has a view or market bias either bullish or bearish, does not have a view (his opinion) that is symmetrical regarding the price movement of an underlying. If your opinion was plotted, it would need to reflect a directional price bias, and probably indicate some relative magnitude of your bias. Keep in mind that the computer modeling in your trading platform does not include your opinion, and even if it did, there is obviously no guarantee it would be accurate. It's always a good idea to be aware of how your software derives its information to plot these graphics. An advanced investor of options needs this basic understanding.

11 Option Spread Trading

Vertical Spreads: Options in the same month but different strike prices

Vertical Spread	Description	Purpose of Spread	Rationale
Call Bull Spread (debit)	Buy a CALL, then sell a higher strike	Profit on move up, minimize time-decay & volatility.	Lower strike price will gain faster than higher strike.
Put Bull Spread (credit)	Sell a PUT, buy a lower strike	Profit on move up, lower risk, minimize time decay and volatility.	Underlying goes up, options expire worthless, keep premium credit.
Call Bear Spread (credit)	Sell a CALL, buy a higher strike	Profit on move down, minimize time decay & volatility.	Underlying goes down, options expire worthless, keep premium credit.
Put Bear Spread (debit)	Buy a PUT, sell a lower strike	Profit on move down, lower risk, minimize time decay & volatility	Higher strike price will gain faster than lower strike.

Some terms, notes, and examples of spreads follow in this section.

More Option Terms:

Combination – An option trade with more than one option. Technically, a combination could be a stock and an option also.

Leg – one side of a combination Placing one of the side at separate times is called legging in.

To **Trade Volatility** – fashioning a trade where part of all of the emphasis is profiting from changes in IV%

Net delta – the algebraic sum of the deltas of a combination (trade)

Vertical spread – a combination using options of the same class (combining strikes above and/or below)

Calendar spread - a combination using options of more than one class

Ratio spread – using options in the same class and not using the same number of options in each leg of the spread.

The terms can be confusing because there may be several names of descriptions of combinations for any one strategy:

Call Bull Spread is also called a **Vertical Call Spread**

Put Bear Spread is also called a **Vertical Put Spread**

A **Call Bear Spread** is selling a Call for a *credit*, then buying a lesser priced strike higher up to be a cap on losses (aka: decrease risk of the trade).

A **Put Bull Spread** is selling a Put for a *credit*, then buying a lower strike Put to be a cap on losses. (aka: decrease the risk of the trade).

All of these trades are **combinations**, and all of these trades are **vertical spreads** – except the calendar spread.

A **credit spread** is a trade where you receive a credit in your account.
A **debit spread** is when your account is debited the cost of the trade.

CALL BULL SPREAD
Also called: Vertical Bull Spread

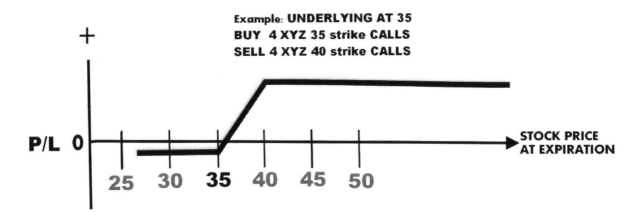

Example: UNDERLYING AT 35
BUY 4 XYZ 35 strike CALLS
SELL 4 XYZ 40 strike CALLS

P/L 0

25 30 **35** 40 45 50

STOCK PRICE
AT EXPIRATION

CALL BULL SPREAD

Description of Strategy: CALL BULL SPREAD (Bullish trade using CALLS)

Break-even: Strike + cost of spread

Buying one CALL and selling a higher strike CALL (debit). The credit received for the higher strike CALL is applied to reduce the cost of the trade, so the trade cost less than just buying a CALL and is less risky. Losses are limited to the nearby CALL premium minus the credit for the higher strike CALL (the cost of the spread). Being long and short the same number of options has the effect of somewhat insulating the trader from IV% fluctuations. This is a debit spread, and the loss is equal to that debit, the net cost of the spread.

Though recommended for advanced traders, it is possible to buy the CALL nearer the money, and then when/if the underlying stock's price goes up, sell the higher strike CALL at that time. This often has the effect of 'locking in' profit to an extent. This is called *legging in the vertical spread* and is more risky because if the underlying decreases (the trade goes against you) before you sell the higher strike, you will not get the credit to offset part of the cost of the spread. In other words, if you are wrong about the bullish price movement, you can't get enough credit from selling the further OTM call to reduce the trade cost significantly.

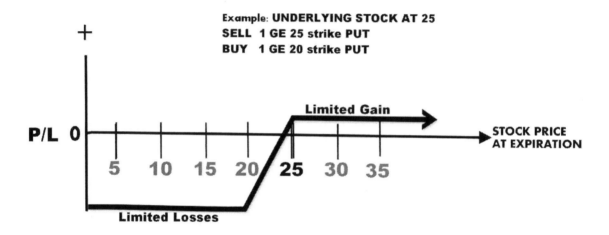

PUT BULL SPREAD

Example: **UNDERLYING STOCK AT 25**
SELL 1 GE 25 strike PUT
BUY 1 GE 20 strike PUT

PUT BULL SPREAD

Description of Strategy: PUT BULL SPREAD (Bullish trade using PUTS)
Break-even: Strike minus the credit amount

Selling a PUT and buying a lower strike PUT for a net credit. The goal is to keep the credit as the options expire worthless, or to exit the trade prior to expiration while keeping a credit. Since you expect the underlying to go up, you can make money if the underlying goes up or stays the same, or even if it goes down by a limited amount. Note that the CALL BULL SPREAD only made money if the underlying goes up. While this trade has a limited profit, it also has less risk. In this trade you are a net seller of options.

CALL BEAR SPREAD

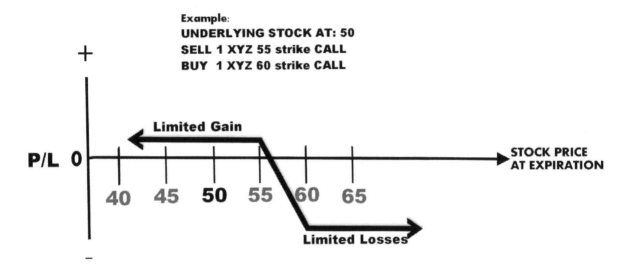

Example:
UNDERLYING STOCK AT: 50
SELL 1 XYZ 55 strike CALL
BUY 1 XYZ 60 strike CALL

CALL BEAR SPREAD

Description of Strategy: CALL BEAR SPREAD (Bearish trade using CALLS)
Break-even: Lower Strike + the credit amount

Selling a CALL for a credit and buying a higher strike CALL to limit losses. You are bearish on the underlying and the goal is to keep the credit for selling the lower strike CALL. You can make money if the stock goes down, stays the same, or goes up a limited amount. This trade is a net seller of options and the maximum profit is the credit you receive when you place the trade. If the options expire worthless, you keep the entire credit.

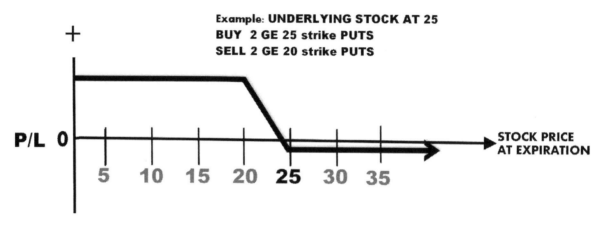

PUT BEAR SPREAD

Description of Strategy: PUT BEAR SPREAD (Bearish trade using PUTS)
Break-even: Higher Strike minus net cost of the trade.

Buying a PUT and selling a lower strike PUT. This is a debit spread. You are bearish on the underlying and you profit as the underlying's price moves down. You only make a profit if the underlying goes down. The profit is limited but this trade is less risky than shorting the stock, or just buying a PUT.

12 VERTICAL CREDIT SPREADS

The two trades featured in this section are ones you need to learn and keep in your toolbox forever; they are the *Vertical Bear Credit Spread* and the *Vertical Bull Credit Spread*. Both pay you money (a credit) up front when you place the trade and if placed correctly, will have a 66% to 98% chance of allowing you to keep that credit without taking any account-slaughtering risks. In this example - the overlay shows that a two-standard-deviations variance – from the underlying's price of 35 - is the exact 'profit zone' of the trade. This illustration is idealized for teaching purposes but it does show how you should consider the profit corridor of trades when choosing strikes.

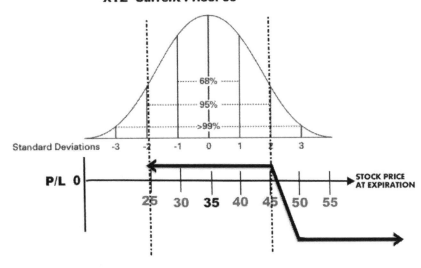

VERTICAL BEARISH CREDIT SPREAD

Example:
SELL 1 XYZ 45 strike CALL for credit of .75
BUY 1 XYZ 50 strike CALL for debit of .30
A NET Credit of (.75 minus .30) = .45 = $45
Maximum Loss: [(50-45) - .45] = 4.55 = $455
XYZ Current Price: 35

This illustration is the Vertical Bear Credit Spread. Here's the setup: The underlying XYZ stock is trading at 35. We are neutral to bearish on the prospects for this stock. Maybe there is a poor earnings report in its news, or maybe it's a stock you have followed for a long time and you think it is near a top and the price is vulnerable, or any one of many other reasons – but our market outlook for this stock is neutral to bearish. The overlay of the standard deviations template indicates that the second SD limits are about $10 above and $10 below its current price at 45 and 25. We know that two SD's covers about 95% of the possibilities in price movement for this stock, and this does not include our bearish market view. Thus, we conclude that our chances for a profit on this trade could be 95% +.

We place this trade by selling a 45-strike CALL for a CREDIT of .75, and simultaneously buying the 50-strike CALL at a *debit* of .30. Our NET CREDIT is .45 or $45. We use the nearby MONTH, so time-value will be on the fast decline. The farther out in time we go to place this trade, the more risky it becomes simply because we are exposing our risk for a longer period of time.

MAXIMUM LOSS: If we are totally wrong on all counts, the stock price zooms up past 50 at expiration and we lose $500, but we still keep the .45 credit, so our MAX risk is $500 less the credit or about $455 less our commissions, which would be less than $4 most likely.

MAXIMUM PROFIT: The CREDIT of $45 (less commissions) is it! So if we define our risk reward: There could be a 95% chance of a profit on this trade and even if the stock goes up $10, stays the same or goes down by any amount at expiration, we still have a profit. Our profit-to-risk ratio is: $45/$455 = or about 10% and if the options expire in 30 days, then a 10% return is pretty nice – annualized about 120%.

This example assumes you hold the position until expiration – and you might. You should also realize, you can close the trade at any time also. If it goes against you and you want out, you'll close it for a loss. But let's suppose the options expire in 30 days, and after 15 days you could close the trade and keep $35, instead of the entire credit of $45. You might choose to take the quick profit and move on; in fact, this is a very common outcome for these type trades. Why continue to risk the trade running back against you, and why risk your $500 to try and keep the other $10? You might also decide that doing nothing but let the options expire worthless is the thing to do; the options could be so far OTM, you are comfortable with taking the 'easy money' – and that's ok too.

Now if you are thinking, this is a lot of trouble just to make $35 or $45, of course you are right. You might have chosen to trade 5 or 10 or even more of the spreads. Selling 10 x $45 = $450, with a max risk of (10 x 500) $5,000 is exactly the same risk/reward ratio. I keep the examples simple is the only reason I used only ONE spread.

If you are going to be a serious option trader, you must learn spreads; they usually give you the most bang for the buck, when considering Prob. of Profit and risk/reward ratio. If you are a beginner, selling naked options with unlimited risk is never advised – this is sort of the 'sky-diving' of option trading; just being wrong once can wipe out your entire account. Using a vertical spread, whether CREDIT or DEBIT, always has a LIMITED risk and not the UNLIMITED risks that you incur when selling naked options.

If you are new to spread trading, remember to use the paper-money mode to practice. It isn't always easy to find the risk/reward that is acceptable to your account size and risk tolerance; you may have to spend some time shopping various stocks and option parameters. Use the trade simulator to practice managing your trade as if it is real money; learning trade management and the 'how and when' of risk management is key to your success. You must not only learn to make money, you must learn to keep it.

I am not suggesting that ideal type trades are always easy to find. There is no substitute for your gaining experience at this type of shopping option prices to mine for good trades. It can be a bit tedious at times, but trust me, you will gain speed as you gain experience. And remember, if you see a trade that 'looks to good to be true', it probably IS! Bid/ask spreads, low open interest, and thinly traded, low volume can have the screen showing you some prices that you might not actually be able to trade. The best computer is the one between your ears, and it will need lots of repetition and practice before your eyes get 'educated' and will spot anomalies in price and volatility patterns.

As wonderful as CREDIT spreads can be, success depends on you selecting the underlying. Some new option traders have extensive stock trading experience and others have very little. For this reason, I will point out for beginners or less experienced traders- that it really pays off for you to have a stable of stocks that you follow regularly, your 'watch lists'. Although it is difficult to make generalities about a specific stock – for the sake of example, I will do it here. It could change by the time you read this book, so do your own homework in real time of course. WMT (Wal-mart) stock seems to make most of its bigger price moves around the NOV to JAN holiday time period. Major retailers quite commonly will make 50% or more of their annual sales in just these three months. Therefore, these are the months with an increased probability of price changes. So if I am going to place a Vertical Bear Credit Spread, I would probably *not* do it at those times of the year with a major retailer like WMT. Conversely, I could check a multi-year chart of WMT and I might find that it has comparatively little price movement during the MAY-JUL time period. Furthermore, I wouldn't place this trade at earnings report time or shortly before. I would place it shortly after the earnings report and expect to be out of the trade in 30 to 45 days prior to the next earnings report; there is less chance for a surprise that could go against my neutral-to-bearish view. If the stock market in general was near a peak, this might also add wind to my sails for the trade. The analyst mode of your trading software can easily plot a stock's price vs. an index, so you can easily check to see if there is a positive price correlation between stock price and an index like the DJIA or S&P500.

I hope this is stating the obvious: Always research the underlying before you place a trade. Learn basic fundamental and technical analysis; this will help you determine various probabilities of price direction and magnitude. Don't force a trade; if one underlying or its option prices are not working – keep shopping for a good trade. This is your job and the more you do it, the better you will get at it. As the wise saying goes: Remember that *not trading:* – CA$H- is a position too!

VERTICAL BULL CREDIT SPREAD

If you are hearing someone build a very bullish case as to why they are buying a stock – and they sound convincing to you, get to your research and check the facts. If you find reason to be bullish also, then take the safe and smart route. Create a vertical credit spread where you can make money even if your market view isn't remarkably correct. Here is the trade with good probability of profit, limited risk, and a decent return on investment considering the short duration of the trade. In this example, the outlook is bullish on the underlying.

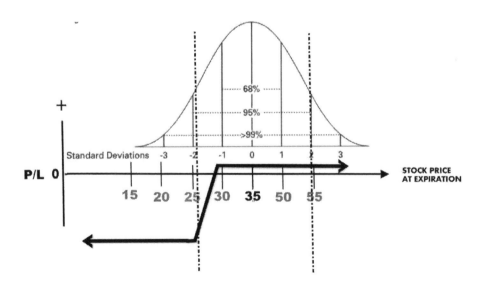

VERTICAL BULL CREDIT SPREAD

Example:
SELL 1 XYZ 30-strike PUT for credit of .65
BUY 1 XYZ 25-strike PUT for debit of .25
A NET Credit of (.65 minus .25) = .40 = $40
Maximum Loss: [(30-25) - .40] = 4.60 = $460
XYZ Current Price: 35

Even though you are bullish, you can make money if the underlying goes up, stays the same, or even if it goes down to a degree. The great thing about vertical credit spreads is that you don't have to be right, you only have to be not completely wrong- and you still make money.

The underlying XYZ is at 35. You sell the XYZ 30-strike PUT for .65 and buy the 25-strike (lower) PUT for .25 for a net credit of .40. The probability of profit as determined by the SD chart is just below one SD at about 68% to 70%. This is not a sure thing by any means. This trade is placed with around 30 days until expiration. Since you are both long and short IV% this trade is somewhat insulated from those fluctuations. Time-decay will be increasing with only 30-days until expiration.

MAXIMUM PROFIT: The credit of $40.
MAXIMUM RISK: $460 (100 shares x $5 per share) less credit = $460

POTENTIAL RETURN: A $40 profit on a risk of (500-40) $460 or about 8.6% return in 30 days or less. That is 104% annualized. If you are paying $1.50 commission per side of the trade, a $3 total, the net profit could be $37, or a return of about 8% or 96% annualized.

ABOUT COMMISSION RATES: You can easily see in this example why these trades are not viable is you are paying $10 per option per side; the commission would take all your potential profits, increase the risk of the trade dramatically, and you will have to pass on these types of trades. Be sure you negotiate low commission rates when you open your account. If you can't get down to under $2.00, keep shopping. Sometimes the account representative you speak to doesn't have the authority to give you the lower rate given your account balance and trade frequency; there are polite ways to ask respectfully to appeal to his or her supervisor. These people work hard and normally will be glad to help you every way possible. If you can work it out, they get a great new customer and you get the lowest commission rate possible.

The VERTICAL BULL CREDIT SPREAD and VERTICAL BEAR CREDIT SPREAD are PASSIVE DIRECTIONAL TRADES. All you have to do to make money is not be wrong.

13 VERTICAL DEBIT SPREADS

VERTICAL BULL DEBIT SPREAD

Example:
BUY 1 KO AUG 40-strike CALL for debit of 1.50
SELL 1 KO AUG 43-strike CALL for credit of .46
A NET debit of (1.50-.46) = 1.04 = $104
Maximum Loss: cost of spread $104
KO Current Price: 40.17
Days until Expiration: 126

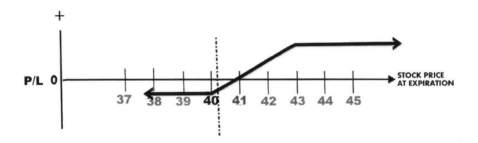

MAX LOSS: Cost of Spread $1.04

MAX GAIN: $300 less cost of spread = $196

NET DELTA OF SPREAD: 0.50 -.21 = .29

BREAK EVEN: Lower Strike + cost of spread = 41.04

An inexpensive way to participate in gains when you are bullish on the underlying. Limited loss, up to 300% gain possible. Time-Decay works against you and IV% is almost neutral.

Trade Management: Initially, with a net delta of .29, expect $29 for each 1.0 increase in the

		Symbol	Price	
Stock:	Coca Cola	KO	40.17	
CALLS	Class	Days until Exp		
	AUG 15	126		
Strike:	Theo Price	Delta	O.I.	Volume
36	4.45	0.93	736	2
37	3.585	0.78	131	0
38	2.77	0.70	673	2
39	2.08	0.61	712	61
40	1.5	0.50	2,571	131
41	1.05	0.39	3,751	10
42	0.71	0.30	4,766	206
43	0.46	0.21	8,117	2061
44	0.3	0.15	19,552	748
45	0.21	0.11	20,266	47

underlying value. KO is a widely traded stock of course; there is plenty of OI and Vol to be able to exit the trade before expiration if you choose to do so. If KO is under 40 at expiration, you lose what you paid for the spread, no more. At expiration, if KO is 41.04 to 43, you make zero to $196. At expiration if KO is 43 and above, you make the maximum net profit of $196.

If the value of this spread increases, you can exit prior to expiration at any time you please. Since time-decay works against this trade, you would prefer to see KO underlying go UP in the first 30 to 60 days. Holding the spread until the last 30 days before expiration means time-decay rate increases rapidly (against you). For example: You might want to hold the trade for the first 60 of the 129 days until expiration, and then if not working for you, take an early exit to avoid having the faster time decay work devalue your spread.

You could have chosen other strike pairs for the same strategy, that I illustrated a 40/43, was entirely arbitrary. The OI and VOL are on the matrix so you can see that these options have liquidity due to their ample OI and VOL. It might be tempting to just buy the 45-strike CALL for .21; it's cheap but the actual probability of this strike being in-the-money is quite remote compared to KO being between 40 and 43. It isn't shown on the chart but the odds of the 45-strike being out-of-the-money at expiration are exactly 90.24%. The probability of the 41-strike being in-the-money (your break-even point) are 38.52%, about 4 in 10 odds. So the spread is 4 times more likely to succeed than the far out-of-the-money 45-CALL buy. Compared with only buying the 45-CALL (no spread); it is true that you only risk $21 and in theory, your profit is UNLIMITED, but that is the same attraction (psychology) as a lotto ticket – and if you insist on playing those odds, over time - it is a poor money management strategy. Look at the OI on the 45-strike at 20,266, the largest of any of the strikes displayed here. Lots of traders love to buy these long-shot options, and you should learn to take their money as often as possible.

This VERTICAL DEBIT SPREAD is not PASSIVE. You must be RIGHT about both price direction and magnitude to make a profit.

Vertical Spreads: Doing the Math

The previous example, the KO 40/43 Bull Vertical (debit) Spread can be a lot less risky than owning the stock. Let's do the numbers: To place the spread, the net cost was only $104; that is only 2.59% of the cost of owning the stock, and the $104 is your maximum loss / worst case scenario on this trade. Let me throw in a caution here. What could make this a good trade or even a great one is NOT the 2.59%, but the fact that IF the stock does rise in the time allotted, the leverage is excellent. The leverage on this trade is much better than just buying a CALL. Just a straight 'buy the CALL trade' pays for all possible rise, not the *most probable* part of the rise. This fact makes the vertical spread more *efficient* than just buying the CALL. The trade-off is that your profits, while more likely, might not be as large. See the next section TRADEOFFS AND RISK ASSIGNMENT graphic for a more detailed illustration.

Vertical Spreads and Your Trading Platform

Recommended Study: If you've already opened your account, go to your trading program (platform) and set it to the practice or paper-trade mode. Pick a stock like KO or WMT, then go to view the option classes and quote matrix. Practice placing a vertical spread trade. The displays will vary depending on your trading software, but find out how to view the quotes on spreads. Normally it is a column display selection. If you need help 'displaying the spread quotes' on the matrix, contact your vendors help. Normally, these screens are set on a default of 'single' option quote displays. You will need to learn to look at spread quotes. While you have help on the line, have them show you how to place an option spread order. Often, your vendor will have a prepared video on this subject, so please ask them where to find it and/or have them email you the link for a training video. Your trading software will display parameters like the net delta of a spread, and other information. The price quotes for the spreads automatically combine the cost of the spread and show you the net premium whether a credit or debit.

VERTICAL BEAR DEBIT SPREAD

Example:
BUY 1 KO AUG 40-strike PUT for debit of 1.51
SELL 1 KO AUG 37-strike PUT for credit of .54
A NET debit of (1.51-.54) = .97 = $97
Maximum Loss: cost of spread $97
KO Current Price: 40.17
Days until Expiration: 126

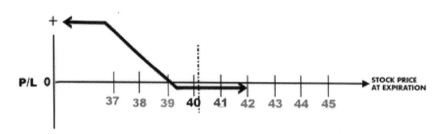

MAX LOSS: Cost of Spread: $97
MAX GAIN: $300 minus cost of spread = $203.
NET DELTA: -.28
BREAK EVEN: 40 less cost of spread = 39.03

Trade Management: This trade is just like the previous trade, the Vertical Bull Debit Spread, except the directional bias is reversed to bearish and PUTS are used instead of CALLS.

		Symbol	Price	
Stock:	Coca Cola	KO	40.17	
PUTS	Class	Days until Exp		
	AUG 15	126		
Strike:	Theo Price	Delta	O.I.	Volume
36	0.37	-0.15	3,254	11
37	0.54	-0.21	5,104	19
38	0.76	-0.28	5,897	72
39	1.07	-0.38	4,176	14
40	1.51	-0.49	6,862	97
41	2.04	-0.61	1,828	2
42	2.70	-0.72	1,432	2
43	3.45	-0.82	1,753	2
44	4.26	-0.90	382	0
45	5.15	-0.98	216	0

14 TRADEOFFS AND RISK ASSIGNMENT

This Vertical Bull Spread will capture the gain of the underlying from 45 up to 50 at expiration. This spread also has a very limited downside (max loss is just the cost of the spread). Owning the stock would have had potentially more profit (**A**) and loss (**B**). So this Vertical Bull Spread has the effect of giving up some gain (**A**) in exchange for reducing the risk (**B**); it is a tradeoff. We can, and do, assign the risk of this trade by choosing the strikes of the options, and shopping the combinations of long CALL and short CALL. We are also able to fine tune our target; in this case the rise in the underlying price between 45 and 50. By choosing the time until expiration (the options class), we also have some control over the time frame of our trade.

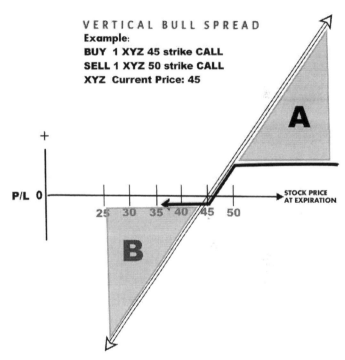

With XYZ at 45, the 45-strike CALL is ATM (at-the-money), and the 50-strike is OTM (out-of-the-money). The 45-strike will cost more than the 50-strike and since we are buying the 45 and selling the 50, this will be a debit spread. The trader has a bullish view and chooses to use this spread because of its limited risk, and the high leverage it provides when compared to buying the stock. The short 50-strike CALL is covered by the long 45-strike, so there can be no margin calls on the trade. If the underlying is 50 or above at expiration, both the calls will be assigned and the stock is effectively bought at 45 and sold at 50 and the trader's account is credited (and the result is *no position* in the stock at expiration). If at expiration, the underlying is between 45 and 50, the trader may exercise the call and own the shares, or sell it for profit. If exercised,100 shares of XYZ at a cost of 45 plus the debit for the trade - and the stock may be sold immediately at the market, *if the traders so instructs*. Almost always the 45 CALL is sold and the profit kept, prior to expiration. If there is a profit in the trade prior to expiration, the trader may close the trade and keep that profit at any time. The net delta of the trade is the algebraic sum of the individual options and will be between 0 and .5; your trading platform will display the net delta both before and during the trade.

Why Spread Trading Options is Key to Your Success

If you've been trading spreads for a while already, you can probably skip this section. *If you are new to spread trading, you must learn right away that trading option spreads is the very bread and butter, the center, the go-to option combinations for option traders.* Many knowledgeable option traders choose not to just buy straight CALLS and PUTS. The reason is simple, spreads are safer, more flexible, affordable, and efficient. I promised you straight talk in this book and right now, I'm telling you if you are going to trade options, concentrate on learning spread trading. Without learning spreads, you are only swimming in the 'kiddie pool'.

If you are a beginner and thought you would start by trading a few CALLS and PUTS don't do it, not yet anyway – I would urge you to learn a little more and then make those decisions. Go ahead in your trade simulation mode, your paper money account – that's fine and a great way to learn. But go ahead and learn spread trading for your real money. By all means, read about them, watch videos, use the trade simulator, and anything else you can find to learn spread trading. When you watch experienced option traders, you will discover quickly just how much better and efficient trade spreads are; experienced traders who know what they are doing - use them all the time. You should use them, practice them, until they are your go-to strategy. Over time, you will begin to understand spread trading so well that it becomes second nature. Spreads allow you to fine tune risks, to focus trades on higher probabilities of success.

15 Passive Directional Trading

The next step in your options education is a step up to the levels of intermediate and advanced trading techniques. If you can't learn to fashion trades and use your new knowledge to be creative, there's a good chance you might not last long in option trading. Learning how to trade options successfully is all about preserving your capital, avoiding large losses, and consistently placing trades with a high probability of profit.

Most professional option traders will agree that entering the realm of **passive directional trading** is the genesis of consistently making money. If there was one section of this book, that I would place in big bold letters in giant red fonts, this is it! *When learning a foreign language, a person reaches a point of fluency that they don't just speak the language or hear it, they begin to **think** in the language.* Beginning and intermediate level option traders must learn the terms and lingo of options, but it is when they accomplish total familiarity with basics that they may advance to using concepts innately. Learning to utilize and embracing the concept of passive direction trading is often the key to consistently making money.

Two of these types of spreads can be defined as *passive directional trading*. In two of the four, the trader receives a credit for placing the trade and there is automatically a trade off for lower risk and lower reward – that yields a high probability of profit:

Call Bull Spread   Put Bull Spread   Call Bear Spread   Put Bear Spread

The *Call Bear Spread* and the *Put Bull Spread* are both examples of *passive directional trading*. The other two strategies in this list only make a profit in one of the three scenarios (up, down, same price movement of underlying) and you must pay a debit (cost) to make the trade. *The Call Bear Spread* and the *Put Bull Spread* win in two of the three outcomes and the trader gets a *credit* when placing the trade.

There are literally scores of options plays (certainly not just the two spreads mentioned) where the principles of passive directional trading are used.

EXTRA DEBIT SPREAD PLAY CONSIDERATION:
A COMMON VARIATION OF A VERTICAL BULL DEBIT SPREAD

Options allow practically limitless creativity; the more you practice and trade –and the more you learn, the better you become.

Here's a problem: You think the stock XYZ is about to have a huge breakout on the upside because of an upcoming earnings report. XYZ stock is $135 a share, so to buy a hundred shares would cost you $13,500, and you could have substantial risks on the downside.

One solution that experienced option traders often use is this use of the Vertical Bull Debit Spread:

Buy a deep-in-the-money 125 CALL, and sell a far-out-of-the-money CALL, the 145-strike as a Vertical Bull Debit Spread. The options (for example) might not expire for 45-60 days out, but you know the earnings estimate is in two days. The 125 CALL is 12.50, and the 145 CALL is 2.00, so the net cost of the spread is: 10.50 ($1050). The most you can lose is $1,050, much less risk than owning 100 shares. If your hunch is right, you could profit from 135 to 145 or $1,000 (if you hold until expiration). If you are wrong, and the earnings announcement is not better than expected, you probably won't lose more than $100 to $300 dollars; most likely you can unwind (close) the trade and take your lumps. The worst case scenario is of course you lose the $1050.

The strategy here is that the 125-CALL, the deep in the money will retain most of its value even if you are wrong over the short term. While the gain is less than buying the stock, so is the risk. Or you may not have had the free funds to use to buy the stock and you still want a play, so you do it with options. Remember a deep-in-the-money option will have a delta between .50 and about .85 – so you stand a chance to make most of the gain without committing the $13,500 to buy the shares.

Recommended Practice Exercise: Select a stock you follow and use your practice-mode-paper-money to shop various strikes and variations of a trade like this. This would be a good time to learn to use the analyze mode of your software, so you can see how this trade will perform over time and at various prices. Hint: You might need help from your vendor the first time you try this. This is a great and fun way to learn option trading.

16 Collars and Synthetics

The COLLAR is handy when you own a stock and you are bearish on it, but do not want to sell it because you might have to pay large capital gains tax. Overall, you are buy-and-hold or for other reasons, you want to keep the stock - but you do not want to suffer losses on the short term. The collar is when (owning the stock) you sell the CALL and use the credit to pay all or part of the PUT cost. The only risk is that you are wrong to be bearish - and your stock prices exceeds the CALL strike. You are 'swapping' most of the downside risk in exchange for what you might have made if you are wrong and the stock goes up above the CALL strike (65).

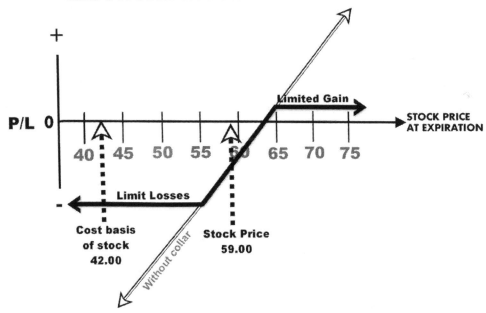

COLLAR

You Own the XYZ Stock at 42.00: Write a covered CALL and buy a PUT
SELL a 65-strike CALL and BUY the 55-strike PUT

SYNTHETIC LONG

Use options instead of buying the stock:

BUY a 60-strike CALL and SELL a 60-strike PUT

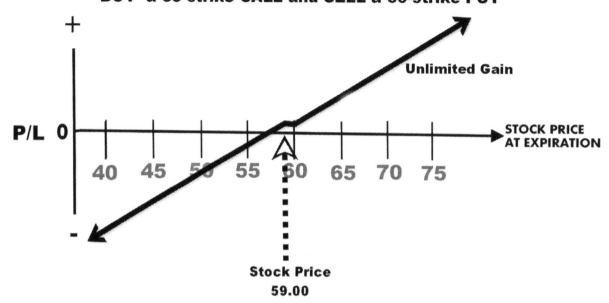

Trading Synthetics

When you have a bullish view on the stock, you can trade a synthetic long stock by buying a CALL and selling a PUT, usually at the same strike (although you can adjust this as you please to alter your risk exposure at various price points). You are going to pay the net premium of the two options and you are going to be required to put up margin money for the naked PUT (which means having that much available in your balance). The margin money will be considerably less than buying the stock outright, but you must keep in mind, if the stock tanks on you, you will be required to cover margin increases. You not only have to be correct about price movement but you must be correct on the timing of the move. A synthetic long stock position would be for a short-term bullish view; it is not a substitute for the long-term buy-and-hold. Another consideration is that the delta of the at-the-money

CALL is only about to be about .50 , so you shouldn't expect the same profit as buying the underlying. There are probably much better strategies to play a bullish bias on a stock, but you need to understand what synthetics are as part of your education.

OTHER SYNTHETICS

Synthetic SHORT stock: The mirror-reverse of the synthetic long: just SELL the CALL and BUY the PUT at-the-money.

Synthetic CALL: BUY the STOCK and BUY a PUT at-the-money

Synthetic PUT: SELL the STOCK and BUY a CALL at-the-money.

Here again, is an opportunity for the terminology to get a bit tangled: A synthetic CALL could be the same as BUYING a PUT on a stock you own to protect the downside. But technically, this term 'synthetic CALL' is not used that way and usually would be used when a trader places both sides of the trade (Buy the stock and buy the PUT) at the same time- to create a synthetic CALL.

Using synthetic CALLS and PUTS is considered an advanced strategy. There are reasons to use them in lieu of an actual CALL or PUT: The delta is 1.0 or -1.0, instead of .50 and -.50 for the CALL and PUT, respectively, so you get quicker gain on the upside, but the trade-off is that you risk virtually unlimited losses on the wrong side of the trade. These are often used in conjunction with advanced strategies and are not uncommon to use in commodity hedge plans where existing inventory (or the need to buy it) can represent the 'underlying' long or short in these trades. Sophisticated commodity traders use synthetics commonly, especially in hedge (price protection) risk management. These are not for beginners, and even intermediate and highly advanced traders could go their entire career and never use them. I put these definitions and terms up, so you can know the terms. Taking a moment to study the basics of synthetics will help you in becoming more fluent in your option trading.

Sing Systems

OPTIONSEXPOSED.NET

17 WEEKLY OPTIONS AND MINI-OPTIONS

Weekly options

The exchanges also list "weekly options series" or "Weekly's". In addition to index weekly options series, the exchanges now participate in a program that allows trading in some equity and ETF weekly options. These Weekly option series are listed along with regular options – and they expire on the Friday's during a month.

As you get familiar with your online trading platform, you will see the weekly's listed along with the regular options. With all the option listings you will see them marked very clearly marked with the 'days until expiration', often in parenthesis. In most online trading platforms, the Weekly's will be color-coded differently than the regular options. If you are unclear, call your broker's help line and ask; they'll be glad to help you.

Weekly's are shorter, sometimes lower-cost options. They are fairly new and were introduced in equities and ETF's only in 2012. They are sometimes used in short term strategies to time a trade in or near news events, earnings reports, ex-dividend dates, and other considerations. Since they have very short lifetimes, these shorter time frames can (not necessarily *do*) offer less risky trades where short term trades are needed for a strategy. These options are physically settled and have the American-style exercise feature; the last trading day for equity and ETF options is Friday. If you have any doubt at all, contact your broker before placing a trade and ask specific questions.

Mini Options

Like the standard 100-share contracts on the same underlying, mini options are 10-share contract American-style options and can be exercised at any time up to expiration at the discretion of the option holder. The Mini Options are not cheaper, they are only smaller and represent 1/10th of the size of the regular (100 share) contracts.

If you are wanting to buy or sell options on a stock that is $900 a share, the regular option might cost as much as $30 per share, or 100 x $30 = $3000 cost for just ONE option. A mini option is for only ten shares and would cost around $300 instead of $3,000.

If you only own 43 shares of a stock and want to write covered calls, you could trade four of the mini-options and use those to write covered calls on 40 of the shares. Likewise, if you own 140 shares, you could write one regular options to cover 100 shares and then four of the mini's for the remaining 40. Note, you won't be paying 1/10th commissions on these; commissions will be full fare.

18 Friendly Advice

I've spent the last twenty-five years as a private consultant helping corporations that buy and sell commodities - set up, monitor, and evaluate their hedge plans, often called *risk management plans*. For more than 50 years, many such companies only used short and long futures contacts to gain the protection they needed from price fluctuations and delivery risks. It wasn't until around 1989 that agricultural options on futures contacts became widely available; this was the same time that personal computing power became widespread and relatively inexpensive. I was in the right place at the right time – and this coming together of modern products, software & computer technology, and the proliferation of online trading was the perfect-storm that launched me into a career where I met and worked with some tremendously talented and generous business people. It is largely due to them, that I am able to write this book and I am inexpressibly grateful for this opportunity.

One Friday morning, just a few years ago (before the first edition of this book) – I met one of my good friends for breakfast. We often talked of our stock trading and option trading, as well as many other interests – as friends do. My friend came to our breakfast with a printout of a form to send an options 'guru' about $3,000 - for a year of trades that guaranteed 95% winners. While I am ignorant about a great number of things, I do happen to be somewhat of an expert on options, so naturally, I wanted to help my friend by showing him how to keep his $3,000 and to execute the types of trades that the guru was promising him. My friend already had a giant head start; he understood basic stock-option trading and that included the language of options – all the terms that beginners must learn.

I was able to take a pen and a few napkins and to go over the basic strategies that this 'guru' was going to offer him for $3,000 a year. Some of the strategies, admittedly, were advanced and probably not common knowledge to most option traders, but neither were they so complicated or that difficult to learn. My friend was a quick study and immediately took one of the three strategies, covered call writing in tax-deferred accounts, and set up a special account and –long story short- managed to add about 15% additional return to that account over the next year. Every time we had one of our breakfast meetings, he urged me to 'write the book' on some of these strategies; both of us are writers and we self-publish our books. I had met him when he attended one of the workshops I teach on self-publishing at the local college.

I had spent the last twenty-five years teaching option strategies and, in other ways, assisting very talented and bright people in industry to construct and monitor the use of options in their risk management plans. I loved the work but had never considered teaching individual online traders some of those same strategies to use in their own accounts – not until my friend repeatedly urged me to do so. And *that* was the genesis of this book.

I learned options the old school way; I read dozens of books and burned midnight oil. There was no internet, no online trading platforms, only lots of books, many of these books costing more than $200 each. The first really powerful options software I bought maxed out my credit card (a fact which I failed to mention to my wife). I was a school teacher and really couldn't afford it, but for some reason I was compelled to keep buying option books, and the most powerful computers and software I could afford.

There is an old adage, "The harder you work, the luckier you get." My luck came in the form of an opportunity. There was a gentleman that heard I was experimenting with new technology for trading agricultural options with computers; he sent me a short message and asked to meet with me. This man was a brilliant hedge strategist who had begun to use advanced option strategies in his hedge/risk management plans at his orange juice processing plant in Florida. He needed someone like me who knew the computer/internet side of option trading and the new software. I was only a conduit for his brilliance in option strategies – and it turned out that the combination of his talents and my knowledge worked very well for his business. In the process, he became my mentor and helped me learn some very advanced risk management techniques, many of those he personally pioneered into the field of applying agricultural options to commercial risk management plans. The late Phil Herndon was my friend and mentor and one of the kindest and most generous people I've ever known. His entire family is equally generous and brilliant. While I was doing work for Phil in Florida, Harvard's MBA school invited Phil to lecture on case studies in commodity risk management. I was fortunate to work on a daily basis with Phil – all while he paid me very well for incorporating his ideas into computer modeled trades. I am an incredibly lucky man to have had such a talented friend and mentor. I wish to thank the reader now for allowing me to tell this story; it is an indulgence - but I wanted to pay tribute to this wonderful man who influenced my life and my family's life - in such a profound way.

Good News for the Reader

The OIC, Options Industry Council, is your friend. It was formed in 1992 and now provides anyone with an internet connection - a full, free, comprehensive, source to use to learn anything about options on equities, ETF's, index, and commodities. These days when something is free, it often means someone is trying to sell you something and the information you encounter is frequently biased. Except for selling you on trading options, the OIC material is non-biased, well-researched, professionally presented, and available 24/7 to learn whatever you want and need to know about options. It is sponsored by exchanges and regulatory agencies to bring forth educational material. OIC may be the strongest, unbiased, most complete place to learn about options ever created. Do not miss the opportunity of making it a resource for learning, advancement, and a user-friendly champion of information.

Distractions

I would advise anyone not to buy option systems, or subscribe to trading services until they have a full basic to advanced understanding of the subject. Once you learn what is going on, some of these services can actually be quite useful. Many are a source of creative strategies and opportunities; just wait until you can tell the difference between these and the 'easy road to riches' chatter. The latter will whet your appetite touting how you can 'get rich working 30 minutes a week', and leave you with less than ideal results. There is no free lunch, but the good news is that when you put in the time, work, and practice – you can get pretty darn good at options trading and find a style that suits your account size, risk tolerance, and that won't make excessive demands on your time.

You sort of pay your 'opportunity cost' up front by investing the time and considerable effort to learn basic and intermediate trading with options. Once you are over that hump, if you are not making at least an average $50 to $100 an hour or more option trading, you are not succeeding at it – and you might move on to something better suited to your talents. You don't have to be any type of math genius to trade options; most of that is done transparently by the trading platform software. As you will see, if you haven't already, the trading platform you use is a very complex, high performance machine. It has more information, features, and screen setups than you will ever need; there is no purpose to learning every detail of what can be done - because you will probably never use as much as half of the features and setups. For this reason, you should avail yourself of the free videos, webinars, and articles on your trading platform. When you view these, you can sort through them to find the one's that will be most useful to you. As long as you continue to explore and learn, you'll be getting better.

In the interest of remaining neutral, I have *not* included a list of reputable well-known trading companies – not in this book anyway. I do discuss some of them on my blog at OptionsExposed.net If you already use a trading platform for stocks, you will probably prefer the familiarity of your existing brokerage company. There is a reason that there are at least half a dozen of these trading companies that have millions of satisfied customers; to state the obvious, different people like different platforms for entirely subjective reasons. If you get to a point where you feel like your existing trading platform is limiting your trading and research, give some of the others a try. To be fair to your existing company, if you just can't figure out how to do something or can't find a feature you need, phone them and explain. Most times, they can easily help you out.

I once had a friend who put in a lot of hours setting up an account, learning her platform, and studying strategies but still couldn't make any money trading options. The solution, as it turns out, was a *can't-see-the-forest-for-the-trees* solution. Her problem had nothing to do with option strategies, it was that she spent so much time on learning to be expert with options, that she failed to remember that 50% (often more) of the trading is *knowing your underlying.* Even in non-directional passive trading, it is paramount to center your trades around equities, ETF's, or indexes with which you are extremely familiar.

How do you follow a stock? Everyone you ask will probably have a different answer; this is fair - as what works for one person might not work for the next. Read stock-picking articles, blogs, TV financial channels, and other sources for information. Make a note of the stock, so next time you go to your watch-list screens, you can add it to your list. Periodically add/remove from your lists; having a list of 100 stocks (at least for me) is pretty useless; I wind up watching only a couple of dozen anyway, often as few as 10 or 15.

The human brain is genetically programmed to look for patterns, we are hard-wired for it. Finding patterns comes natural to us. Let this part of your brain do its work. After you follow a stock for a while, read news on it, watch the chart on it, and see how it behaves in context of other indicators and stocks, you may begin to feel familiar with it. If you are an entirely left-brained person, this may not make much sense to you, but I urge you to give it a go and see what happens. There are traders who use either technical or fundamental analysis; the technical being chart indicators along with price bands of resistance and support – and the more fundamental approach of spreadsheets, earnings, and the study of trends and business segments. A large group of traders use both; I am in this segment. When asked, I recommend a balance of the two, the technical and fundamental.

If you or someone you know - has a background in a particular business or type of business, then use every opportunity to capitalize on that knowledge. You can sometimes find good ideas by asking other investors what they like and why, but also verify information others give to you. When others give you advice, they will often maximize their successes and forget to mention the losers; it's just human nature.

Mistakes

Most of us are taught from the time we are babies that it always pays to be optimistic and to spin things positive whenever we can. That same advice can kill your investment account balance! Any denial you practice can have you holding a losing hand too long, and then, if you switch to the *it can't get any worse before it gets better* mode, you are really in trouble. That's like double-denial.

If half of option trading is knowing your underlying, then half of your money management is recognizing the fact that you will not have 100% winners.

Just as you must formulate a plan for when to take a profit, you must have a preset notion of when a trade is not working for you. Before you hit the SEND button to open a trade, ask yourself, "Do I have a best-case, worst-case, and a *take-the-profits* scenario for each trade? Do I have an exit plan, if things don't go my way?" Even when you do your best, you will still wind up getting out too soon on some trades - and too late on the others. Unless you can tell the future - this is unavoidable. Don't beat yourself up; such perfection is impossible. A cardinal rule: Plan every trade with the primary goal of surviving to trade another day.

Surprisingly, one of the natural *reluctances* we have is to take profits on a good trade; this can also destroy you. New stock traders often experience this. Everyday a stock goes up, you feel smarter and smarter, and you enjoy counting your profits, UNTIL one day the trade turns on you. Then you want it to be 'good again' and hold it, and then lose more. Any stock trader that won't admit to having done that – isn't being totally honest. Losing in the best possible way does not come natural to any of us; yet if you are going to survive it's a necessary skill to learn.

I read an article once by a proclaimed successful stock and commodity trader. His mantra was: "Cut your losses quickly and let your profit run or you will never survive!" His mantra sounded good (Everybody loves profits, right?) but was impossible to do without clairvoyance. It reminded me of the old comedian Will Rogers who said this about stock investing – except he intended it to be nothing more than tongue-in-cheek humor. He said, "Buy low, sell high. If they don't go up, then don't buy them." Such arbitrary and unquantifiable rules are little more than wishes cast into the air. Another credo often sited by rookie stock investors is to 'buy more while its going up'; this can have you averaging in for the next correction (what I call the *Icarus Syndrome*.) Always question these 'parrot phrases'; if you keep an open mind, sometimes people will try to fill it with junk.

Paper Trading

Use the trading simulation features (aka: paper trading) of your online trading platform. You will learn a lot more than just option strategy by doing so. There comes a point where using your trading platform becomes transparent, like the way you are aware of your fuel gage and speedometer when driving even though you don't really think about doing it. The nice thing about using the simulator is that you can't lose any money; the worst thing about using your trade simulator is you can't lose any money. (You read that correctly). When you remove all fear and consequence from trading, as with these simulators, you are missing vital components of your training – specifically, how to deal with the results.

If you are new to all this, spend your first few days or weeks just learning how to use the features of your trading platform. As you get comfortable – start keeping score with your pseudo balance. Trading play money will never simulate real world trading completely but it is among the very best of all ways to learn to trade. The reason I suggest you learn the trading platform first, is that learning the platform and learning option trading at the same time is less than ideal; your attention will be divided. It's a bit like the first time you tried to drive a car; you had no experience and you felt like you had to remember and do twenty things at once; the cure for this malady is practice. You don't have to be an expert before moving on to real trading, but you should reach a certain comfort level and not constantly be searching or losing your place. The quickest, fastest path to learning your trading platform is to practice.

All the online trading platforms will display probable stock price charts - based on the volatility of the underlying stock. The probability of options ITM/OTM at various dates during a trade - is also an important feature to seek out; this might be labeled an 'analytical' view or something similar. Learn to use these features to view 'what if' scenarios like: "If XYZ stock goes up $10/share in 35 days, what will my trade be valued?" or "If XYZ shares go down $3/share in 15 days, how much could I lose?" These sorts of scenarios are not exactly for the beginner, but these will become easier with practice –and over time, may become indispensable trade management tools for you. Using these instruments is very similar to the control panel of an aircraft pilot; without them you could be flying blind. Virtually all professional traders are acutely aware of these parameters as they trade; it becomes a pattern of thinking.   Professional option traders over time, get where they can do these computations in their heads almost intuitively. Again, I'll remind you that asking for help from your customer service is not a weakness; it is a way to save you from wasting time. The software platforms for online option trading have so many features that are not intuitively obvious – that you will need help from time to time. Speed your learning curve by finding and using the free training material they provide.

After you have viewed hundreds of option matrices over time, your brain will get trained to spot anomalies in the patterns of the various parameters like delta, theta, IV%, price, bid/ask skews- and so on. When you get to this level, you will get a quantum leap in creativity in option trading. This is not something you must do, but if you keep at it - over time – your brain becomes trained – but it takes hundreds of hours of experience to get there. These are the hard-earned tools that professional veterans have that most traders never accomplish. *You may be familiar with: 10,000 Hours of Practice. In the book Outliers , author*

Malcolm Gladwell says that it takes roughly ten thousand hours of practice to achieve mastery in a field. This is the type of time it takes for total mastery of a complex subject, but you don't need anything near 10,000 hours to become a decent trader; thousands of new option traders do it every month.

Find Your Comfort Zones

You should know that you won't have to be good at thirty, twenty, or even ten option strategies in order to make money. There is a myth that the more complicated a strategy, the more you can make – but it simply isn't true. Quite the opposite really, simple is usually better. After you accomplish the most basic tasks of option trading and are comfortable with your trading platform, I high recommend you learn to trade Vertical Credit Spreads. These trades are passive non-directional, meaning you don't have to be right about the direction or magnitude of the underlying's price. This strategy will give you - at least in theory - a 66% chance of a profitable trade from the get-go. But there is a less obvious and quite logical reason these trades can work well: They are easier to manage than active directional trades. Another way to say this is: When the vertical credit spreads aren't working, it doesn't (usually) hurt as much, so they are easier to manage. They generally move slow or at least slower. Since vertical credit spreads (and debit spread too) use two strikes with one long and the other short, the combined delta is (usually) lower than the active directional trade. After all, in a directional active trade, you start off in the hole - but with passive non-directional trades, you start off ahead (with a credit not a debit). Online individual traders that are paying very low commissions (as little as 65 cents to $1.50 per leg per side) can make trades that traders paying $10 per leg per side – can't even consider. The good news is that these trades will have a high probability of success, commonly 85% and higher. The 'bad news' is that you won't make a killing doing these trades. It is the quintessential trade off, lower risk = lower gains. I will caution you, that you must learn to kill these trades quickly if they aren't working; one bad one - can take away the low profits of several good trades – and this is demoralizing, but still it happens sometimes. If some advanced traders are reading this, they may think my warning wasn't strong enough. You really do have to manage these trades carefully. For the advanced readers, I will also state that using an underlying with high volatility (not IV% of the option - but historical volatility of the stocks itself) is statistically less successful than using an underlying with lower volatility. The reason is that the nominal distribution of probability curve will have 'flat tails' and be less predictable. This expression, 'flat-tails' is meant to convey the phenomenon of the probability distribution out past two standard deviations - dropping to zero *slower* than some option-modeling software predicts. In plain language, this merely means that highly volatile stocks are less predictable. Add to this the fact that the farther OTM an option (all else being equal), the higher it's IV% becomes.

Don't become obsessive with your trading. I once wanted to manage an investment commodity fund; I worked hard, raised the money from investors, and a few months later I realized I had become the stereotypical, compulsive screen watcher who had no time for fun or family. I am ashamed to admit this, but I think (now with the full advantage of hindsight of course) it as an important part of my trading education. I was at the screen all day and half the night, and when I wasn't there, I was thinking about being there. My life had no life; I was addicted. It's all about balance, no matter if the trading is going well or not; though I will tell you when the trading is going very bad, it is quite a hellish existence. After my bout with my phase of 'serious trading', I realized that trading often, conducting many, many trades per day – had drastically diminished my success. I suppose at some level, it had been drilled in my head – perhaps as a child – that if 'trying' a thing is good, then 'trying it more' is always better. Well, this simply isn't true. I also used to think that the harder a person works, the better and more successful they become, but unless you build widgets and get paid by the piecework, this isn't true either.

The third degree of this type of thinking is that working hard will guarantee rewards 100% of the time. Like you, I know people that work incredibly hard and wind up with nothing, all the time beating themselves up because they think they failed because they should have worked even harder. I am all for hard work and believe in its necessity, but you must learn to work smart and find the right tools- for only working hard doesn't guarantee you anything. I am a Steve Jobs fan, and I read the story that explains why he likened computers to be a 'bicycle for the brain'; the bicycle is one of the most efficient means of human powered propulsion.

If you aren't making money, change something. Einstein said that doing the same thing over and over and expecting different results is the very definition of insanity. Trade sanely!

Keep Learning. You got where you are by being smart, willing to work, and by learning more than you *had* to. Option traders are in a minority; you are different in some very unique ways. Don't trade like it's a hobby, trade to make money. If you enjoy learning, you will love option trading. I have fun with it and find satisfaction; I hope you will also. I sometimes think of sitting down at my trading platform as a sort of video game that pays good money when I play – and that is something I enjoy doing immensely.

Think Like a Professional. Personal investing is a business; make your decisions to help your company thrive. Insist that changes are made until you find ways to make it work. You ARE the CEO!

Congratulations! You are now on your way. You have the basics and more – and know where to go and how to begin. Thank you for reading this book.

I lived in West Texas for a while in my youth. I learned some colorful language there, a lot of it I can never repeat in a book like this one. One thing I remember that helps me trade better is an old West Texas saying that all fathers teach their sons and daughters: "Never miss a good chance to shut up!" It reminds me that sometimes the best thing to say is nothing, and I can tell you from experience that sometimes, the best trade you do is 'nothing'. Timing is everything and often it is the trades *we don't make* that protect the money we have made and allow us to keep it for another, better, time.

Thank again for reading my book. I wish you every success and enjoyment possible.

Cautionary Words

There's an old adage: Beware of strangers bearing gifts. As a rule, don't buy penny stocks, binary options, or run out to pay someone you never heard of a few hundred dollars a month to feed you trades 'guaranteed to win'. Iron Condors can be a great strategy, and so can trading Weekly options; I'm only saying give yourself a chance to get up to speed before you make those decisions. All of us want shortcuts; we want ways to riches that don't require education, work, and our valuable time. Do your homework, research methods, get references and talk to other traders before you leap into a shortcut. Use your common sense, if someone had a truly easy path to riches, why would they sell it for a few hundred dollars? Why don't they just surround themselves with traders and split the profits and risks with them? They would make a lot more money and people would be beating a path to their door to do it. They wouldn't be advertising to sell their 'systems'. All they would have to do is to help a dozen of their friends get rich, and then everybody who heard of it would be glad to sign up. These types of offers (IMHO) are like the email from Nigeria that wants to give you free money, and then requests only a small deposit in return. If it's too good to be true, it probably is.

I have on my desk in front of me at this very minute an envelope from a self-proclaimed options guru. Next to my name and address on the outside of the envelope is says in big bold letters: **DO YOU HAVE 9 MINUTES A WEEK TO DOUBLE YOUR INVESTING INCOME?** This fellow in the enclosed material says, "Give me 9 minutes a week and I guarantee You $80,000 a year." I did the math and if what he says is true, you'll make $10, 256.41 cents per hour on the average! This guy claims he went to Yale, has a Harvard MBA, and will share his secrets with you for the equivalent of $1.90 a day ($697 per year, discounted from the regular rate of almost twice that). He says he knows 'secrets' and he touts his use of **credit spreads** and a timing system - as keys to his success.

My book cost you about the price of a pizza. I mentioned earlier that I had lived for a while in my youth - in West Texas – and picked up some colorful expressions there. When a fellow promises you over $10,000 per hour for almost zero effort, it reminds me of one of those West Texas sayings: "Don't piss on my boots and tell me it's raining." This is the reason I named my book **Options Exposed**. There is no secret. There is only knowledge, practice, experience – and money to be made.

"Many a small thing has been made large by the right kind of **advertising**." -**Mark Twain**

19 Resources

OIC Options Information Council

URL: **OptionsEducation.org** This is a must site for option traders. Caution: There are no less than a dozen websites who will try to hijack your browser by clever search engine listings of similar names; may sure you have the real Options Information Council.

OptionsExposed.net

This is my blog. You'll find free articles and discussions on strategies – and the fine points of spread trading. I try to supply ideas to help you learn and explore option trading. If you want to sign up for email notifications of new articles, trading tips, and links to educational material on options, just write me at **Don@WriteThisDown.com** and put "OE" in the subject line. You'll be able to cancel at any time from my mailing list, and privacy is guaranteed. I also welcome ideas and questions for future articles and suggestions on how this book can be more helpful in future editions. Thank you.

Sing Systems
OPTIONSEXPOSED.NET

Free Training Programs

OIC.com

CBOE.com

OCC.com

I also have a list of some online trading companies that you can shop – and more resources on the list of web sites where you can find good material and training. I do not recommend one over another and do not have any financial relationship or reward of any kind by listing these; it's just a list for you to check out and see if any suit your preferences. I do try to list most of the majors that offer great platforms and very low commissions.

If you wish me to consider posting information about a specific trading company on my blog - just send me an email and maybe I can share your information with readers of the blog. Thank you. Don@WriteThisDown.com

I do recommend, that when you open an account, you take every advantage of the trading videos and websites of your trading company. The videos and material on how to use their respective platforms is extremely helpful. Almost all of them have very skilled people to help you in every way possible. It is a very competitive industry and they want to make and keep you satisfied with their products. Please check out my blog at: OptionsExposed.Net

Sing Systems

ADVANCED STRATEGIES FOR EXPERIENCED TRADERS

The remainder of the playbook of strategies are for advanced and experienced option traders. Become familiar with them as they help you with your options education. Nothing about these strategies automatically makes them 'better' or 'worse' than the strategies already covered. Don't assume just because they are 'advanced' that they are more likely to make you any money. Most traders that use these strategies still rely heavily on the spread trading already covered by this book. Of course you need to learn and use them, and most of them are only modifications of regular spread trading. Some of these strategies rely heavily on the trader having an advanced understanding of IV%.

One thing you will surely want to do is to look up these strategies at OIC (and other sources) and pursue more details on how they may be used.

20 Strangles and Straddles

LONG STRANGLE

A LONG STRANGLE is a combination trade that BUYS an equal number of out-of-the-money CALLS and PUTS. The trader pays for both options with no credits to offset the purchase premiums of the options. The profits are made if and when the underlying has a breakout in either direction. You can lose on this trade if the underlying stays the same, or if it moves up or down but not enough to be profitable. This is one of the most impossible scenarios to make money options trading; this is because you are paying for the price breakout but the strategy buys both directions (double the cost of an option or spread that has directional bias). In addition to that difficulty, a decrease in IV% will speed the decay of your options premiums. If you try to place the long strangle when volatility is low, this will work in your favor. Altogether, to make money with this trade you have to not let decreasing IV% sink you, and you have to overcome two option prices before you get to any profit, AND you have to get the timing correct. That a lot that has to go right. This trade is the opposite of passively directional trading. Be very careful; this is always a risky one.

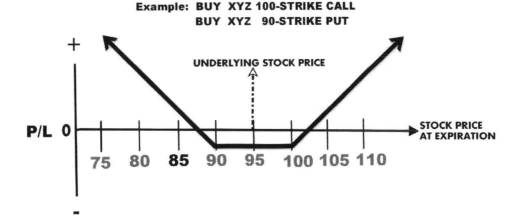

LONG STRANGLE

Example: BUY XYZ 100-STRIKE CALL
BUY XYZ 90-STRIKE PUT

SHORT STRANGLE

The SHORT STRANGLE is a combination trade that SELLS an equal number of out-of-the-money CALLS and PUTS for a credit. The ideal time to place this trade is when your market view is neutral and IV% is at/near a peak. You should remember that when IV% is high, the options are most expensive – the ideal time to SELL them. You also must remember you have virtually (in theory) unlimited risk exposure with this trade. Ideally the underlying will rattle around in your profit corridor as time-decay decreases the short options value, and you also would like to see the IV% on the decline to further decrease the premium of your short options.

I cannot emphasize enough how you need to analyze the underlying thoroughly. A stock with a high beta (a high correlation to the general market conditions) adds risk to this trade; conversely, a low beta could be in your favor. And it is imperative you know the earnings forecasts, the earning announcement dates, and any other news that could unexpectedly sway the stock price. One way to statistically lower your risk exposure on this strategy is to not use options with long periods until they expire; the less time you are exposed, the better this trade might be.

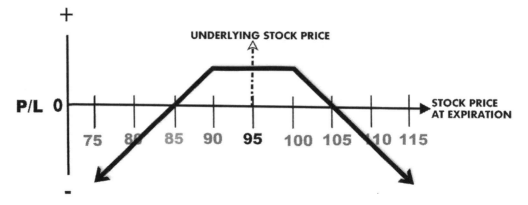

SHORT STRANGLE

Example: SELL XYZ 100-STRIKE CALL
SELL XYZ 90-STRIKE PUT

Another unique characteristic of the SHORT STRANGLE is that it *does not* require margin for each leg of the trade- but only for one of them; this is because you do not risk both outcomes at expiration- either, but not both outcomes are possible.

When placing a SHORT STRANGLE, you should learn to read the IV% in the options classes' matrix. When you see unusually high IV% skews, check to see if there is some news or other information about which you are unaware. The IV% skews and spikes can tip you off to such things. Once you find the source of these things, you stand a chance of using them in your favor, perhaps by modifying strategy, strikes, or other factors. Events like earnings reports, takeovers, merges, and buyouts are just a few things that can be source of patterns in IV%.

When I sat down to write this book, I was going to write a simple book just outlining option strategies, but I realize quickly that unless there is constant discussion of how the strategies work (and can be used) in conjunction with the underlying – it would be a case of 'a little knowledge is dangerous'.

THE IRON CONDOR

The names of some option strategies can be very visceral: strips, spreads, splits, strangles, straddles, puts, and calls. If there was ever a strategy that named out of sci-fantasy, it is the IRON CONDOR. In most option books, the iron condor is tucked away in a final chapter written for veteran, seasoned, experience, battle-tested option traders. Before computers, online trading, and highly sophisticated trading platforms became common, I might have agreed to hide this strategy on a back page, but not any more.

Study the previous SHORT STRANGLE. By just adding two options, it turns into an IRON CONDOR, also known as a SHORT CONDOR. The riskiest part of the SHORT STRANGLE is the fact that possible losses far OTM are virtually unlimited; the IRON CONDOR has fixed *limited* losses. I going to use the same trade example but I will add a LONG 85-strike PUT, and a LONG 105 CALL to the trade – and this will convert the trade (from the short strangle) to an IRON CONDOR.

Now compare the SHORT STRANGLE P/L chart to the IRON CONDOR:

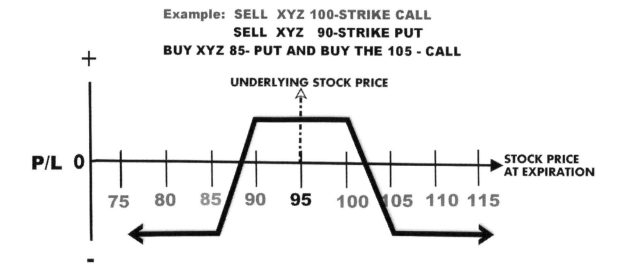

The only thing about an option trade that should be truly intimidating is exposure to large and/ or unlimited risks. Trades can go bad when you least expect it, and the result can be most deadly to your account balance. Plus, you have to keep your morale and confidence up – and that's almost impossible when you suffer one or two large losses that wipe out weeks or even months of good trading. I think it is just as important to protect your confidence as it is to protect your account balance. If you are trading and your progress runs in streaks between catastrophic losses, you need to get another plan; the one you are using isn't working.

You must trade in your comfort range – and this means applying strategies where you understand all aspects – best case, worst case, break-even, and exposure to various kinds of risk (IV%, news, earning reports, and others). It also means you must know that any one particular trade will not destroy your balance or your confidence. Your work doesn't end when you place the trade, that is only the beginning. You must learn to manage each of your trades, often this means you need to know how to end this quickly if necessary – and to be 'ok' with that. I'm not saying 'maybe' this will happen; I'm telling you it is a certainty and you should be prepared emotionally and mentally to pull that trigger when you need to do so. Managing your trades is a skill like learning to drive; you can read about it for year and you still can't do it. You must put in time behind the wheel and get comfortable with making constant adjustments to have a smooth and safe ride. So if you are a beginner and on your way to more sophisticated trading, select trades that you can handle whether they turn out good, bad, or ugly. Work your trade management skills and confidence at your own pace.

Years ago when I first started trading commodities, I was ahead on one of my first trades and quite satisfied it had gone just the way I wanted. My profits were running up. So I went to lunch and when I got back, my account was down by several thousand dollars, $4,522 exactly. Sometimes I hate being good at math; I instantly knew my lunch had cost me $75 a minute! And that one trade wiped out profits on the last five in a row. I exited the trade, took the losses, and then turned all the equipment off and spent the rest of the afternoon licking my wounds and thinking maybe this commodity stuff isn't for me. If I had been worth millions, losing that amount might not have hurt so much, but I was a teacher at a technical college and that was about a month's pay. I urge you to plan your trades and above all never put yourself in the position to lose a chunk of money that will make you feel like I felt that day, and for the few days that followed. Be defensive. Be careful. You are number one; look out for 'number one' above all else when you trade.

LONG STRADDLE

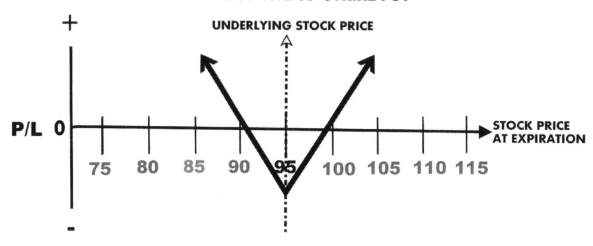

LONG STRADDLE

Example: BUY XYZ 95-STRIKE CALL
BUY XYZ 95 -STRIKE PUT

The LONG STRADDLE is placed by simultaneously buying a CALL and PUT at the same ATM strike. It is not profitable at expiration until the cost of placing the trade is offset by a move in either direction of the cost of the trade. This strategy can backfire quickly if you pay too much for options. A trader might hold a view that the underlying is due a breakout in one direction or the other. It is quite possible, other traders may be thinking the same, and if this is true, the options may be already trading with a high IV%; that means they could be too expensive; you can literally be 'right' and still lose money. Buying in this scenario is risky; if the IV% suddenly declines, the options can lose premium quickly. Anytime you hold long option positions, there is time-decay working against you already. It might sound good to think you have an option play that 'makes money whether the underlying goes UP or DOWN, but there is a lot more going here than only that. The very thing (volatile price movement of the underlying) that makes this breakout play attractive can also be what makes placing this trade prohibitively expensive (due to the high IV% and high price of the options). If you see an opportunity where the options are reasonably priced, and see higher IV% coming up, this play is one way to buy volatility with the view that the stock is due a breakout in either direction. These days, you probably won't have any news the rest of the market hasn't already factored into the price of the underlying and the options. This strategy can require close monitoring and the timing for success can be very critical; this is why this strategy is recommended for only highly skilled and experienced option traders.

Description of Strategy: Long Straddle: Simultaneously buying the same number of at-the-money CALLS and PUTS.

Break-even: Strike + premium paid OR Strike minus the premium paid

SHORT STRADDLE

Example: SELL XYZ 95-STRIKE CALL

SELL XYZ 95 -STRIKE PUT

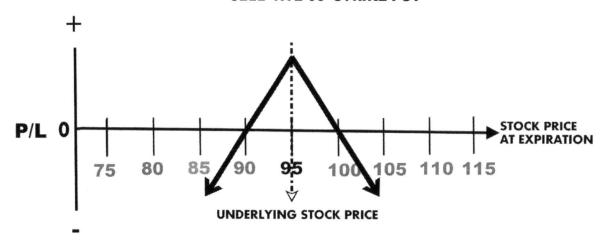

SHORT STRADDLE

Description of Strategy: SHORT STRADDLE: Price-neutral, sell ATM CALL and PUT

Break-even: Strike, plus or minus the credit amount

This is a strategy not recommended for beginners or even intermediate traders. The strategy sells at-the-money CALLS and PUTS at the same strike (an equal number of each). There is unlimited risk in both directions, and inherently this strategy will lose one side of the other if held until expiration.   The SHORT STRADDLE could be used to sell volatility, with time decay working in the trader's favor; note that neither of these mitigates the risk of big losses if the underlying has a price breakout in either direction. For those reasons, this one is for very advanced and experienced traders, and could easily require expert timing and requires close monitoring.

21 Ratio Spreads

Ratio spreads are a must for intermediate and advanced option traders; they allow a trader to virtually fashion a custom curve for almost any P/L . There's more good news: When you use your online trading platform, you will find it has easy methods of placing these trades, it computes the debit or credit automatically, and you can use the analytic features to graph the P/L for you over time.   You recall (or already know if you are an experienced trader of course) that many options and option trades are not held until expiration; your trading platform software can give you any snapshot in time – of how your trade might develop. For example: You might put on a ratio spread using options that expire in 71 days; you can use the graphical analytics of your trading software to show you scenarios at 14 days, or anytime until the options expire.   Your trading platform software can run various trade scenarios for values of IV%; this gives you a way to understand how the trade might fare under various market conditions – and see how changing IV% affects trades. You might want to know how your trade will look in 30 days with a 20% increase in implied volatility (IV%). Your software can plot this and display all underlying price scenarios at the same time.

Until just a few years ago, the power you have now furnished free by your online trading company, was not readily available to small investors due to its high cost and complexity. Now you get it free, plus you have virtually unlimited help by chat, phone, online lessons, and videos.   The advances in computer power and on-screen displays makes all these operations easier than they have ever been before.

This online trading software (as mentioned before) has a paper money mode, where you can run your trade ideas, just as pilots train on flight simulators. This trade simulation run in real time - is probably the greatest option teaching tool ever invented; you have full support and unlimited trials and lesson available to you. Use them and you will become fluent with option strategies ten times faster than you might without doing so.

SHORT RATIO CALL SPREAD

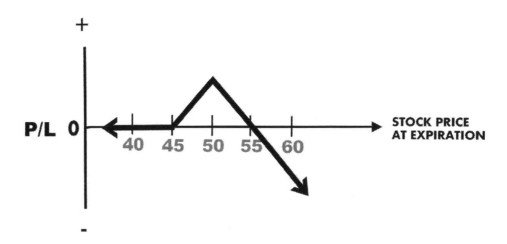

SHORT RATIO CALL SPREAD

Description: The same as a vertical bull CALL spread + a naked CALL. Buy the 45 CALL, and by selling two of the 55 CALLS you get enough premium credit to pay for the lower strike (45) CALL. This trade can often be placed with a small credit or near breakeven (as the example in the graph above). A small rise in the underlying price and/or falling IV% work in favor of this trade.

Example:
LONG 1 XYZ 45 CALL
SHORT 2 XYZ 50 CALLS

Obviously if XYZ is trading at-the-money for the LONG 45 CALL, the trader expects some short-term upside in the underlying stock. Notice the theoretical unlimited loss out past 55; the trader should be very informed when placing this trade --- a surprise higher-than-expected earnings report, or other news could turn this trade against you quickly. Clever strategies are great and offer flexibility some risk controls, but without good research on the underlying – these trades should never be placed.

LONG RATIO CALL SPREAD

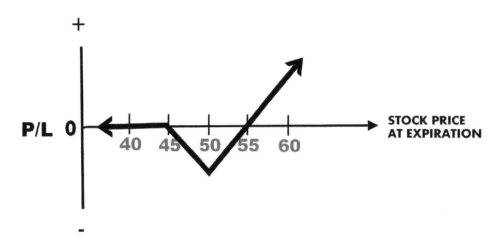

LONG RATIO CALL SPREAD

Description: Short an at-the-money CALL and then buy two higher strike CALLS. The volatility play on this trade is that you are net long IV%. Profit from sharp increases in IV% and/or underlying price.

Example:
SHORT 1 XYZ 45 CALL
LONG 2 XYZ 50 CALLS

The trader not only has to be right about price direction but also the move up has to be significant; notice the worst-case on this trade is when the underlying goes up $5. This trade has significant risks to it. Any increase in IV% will probably assist the trade and time-decay works against the trade.

LONG RATIO PUT SPREAD

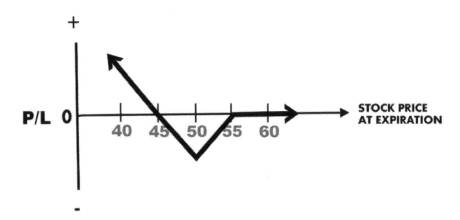

LONG RATIO PUT SPREAD

Description: Short 1 PUT and long two PUTS with a lower strike. The strategy is like a bull put spread + a long PUT. The market view is for a sharp decline in the underlying and/or a sharp move higher in IV%. The combined delta of the two long PUTS is about the same as the short PUT when the trade is initiated.

Example:
SHORT 1 XYZ 55 PUT
LONG   2 XYZ 50 PUTS

This is an aggressive trade as a stand alone; not only must the investor be correct about the underlying's price movement but also the magnitude and timing.

SHORT RATIO PUT SPREAD

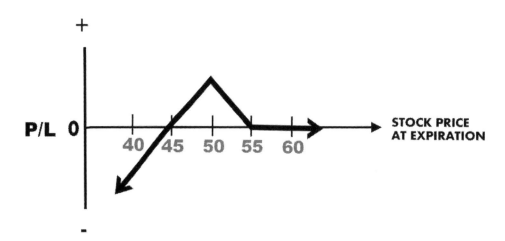

SHORT RATIO PUT SPREAD

Description: Buying an at-the-money PUT and selling two PUTS with a lower strike. It is like a bear put spread plus a naked PUT. The trader expects a small trading range and/or a significant fall in IV%.

Example:
LONG 1 XYZ 55 PUT
SHORT 2 XYZ 50 PUTS

This is usually a delta-neutral trade; when it is placed with other ratios, 2x3 or 3x5, it is called a ***Christmas tree*** spread. As time passes, the premium decay (time decay) of the short PUTS can build profits but only so long as the underlying trades in a very limited range. The maximum profit is if the underlying is at the is at the lower PUT strike at expiration. If placed at even money or even a small credit, the investor can make money if the underlying trades in a limited range or goes up, and the trade profits from decreasing IV%.

COVERED RATIO CALL SPREAD

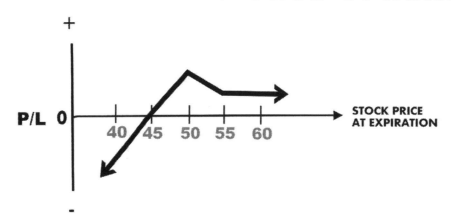

COVERED RATIO CALL SPREAD

Description: Also called a Covered Combination, this trade is a long stock , and short two CALLS at one strike – and long one CALL at a higher strike. Increasing IV% has a negative impact on this trade; time-decay works in your favor.

Example:
LONG 100 shares of XYZ SHORT 1 XYZ 45 CALL
SHORT 2 XYZ 50 CALLS
LONG   1 XYZ 55 CALL

This trade is used to earn additional money while owning shares of the underlying stock. Sometimes investors will use this trade on a stock to decrease the cost basis of the stock. The investor can profit if the stock range-trades, goes up, or goes down slightly. The losses would actually be due to the stock and not the options, which is a risk that was already there if you held the long stock. If an investor is behind on the stock purchase, this trade is sometimes used to reduce the cost basis of the stock. Be concerned about dividend payments (dates), and other news.

As a general rule, it is usually not wise to try and convert a bad trade into a good trade by adding on options. Adding options in mid-trade is sometimes done to lock-in some of the existing profits. There are exceptions to every rule of course, so think it through; it's usually not a good idea to add risk to a losing trade.

22 Condors and Butterflies

Description: Four different strike CALL options. You may think of it as an in-the-money bull call spread and an out-of-the-money bear call spread combined. The strategy is one where the investor expects little movement in the price of the underlying. The greatest profit is when, at expiration, the underlying is between the two short CALLS.

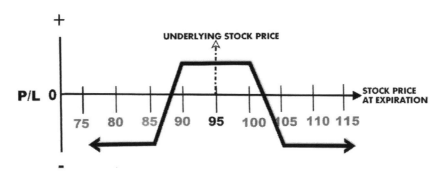

LONG CALL CONDOR

Example:
LONG 1 XYZ 85 CALL
SHORT 1 XYZ 90 CALL
SHORT 1 XYZ 100 CALL
LONG 1 XYZ 105 CALL

The example here has $10 between the two short CALL strikes (90 and 100); when you place a wider distance between these strikes, the probability of profit goes up, but the maximum profit goes down (risk vs. reward trade off). The investor thinks the underlying will remain between the two short CALL strikes during a specific time period. The maximum risk of the trade is the net debit you pay for the trade. *There is risk of assignment in this trade (the strike of the lowest long CALL can be in-the-money) so the investor may be required to borrow or finance the stock for one business day. The investor can avoid this by closing out the trade.*

LONG PUT CONDOR

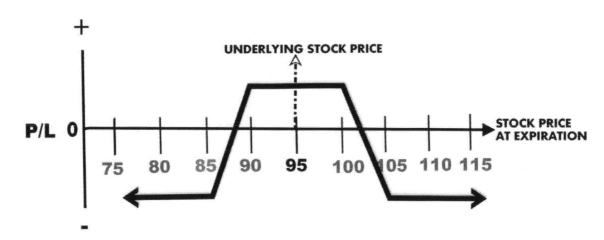

LONG PUT CONDOR

Description: The same as an out-of-the-money bull put spread (at the lower strikes) and an in-the-money bear put spread (at the higher strikes).   Maximum loss is $500 minus the debit.   The maximum gain would occur if the underlying security is between the two short put strikes at expiration. In that case, the higher strike long put is worth its maximum value. The profit would be the difference between the strikes less the premium paid to initiate the position.

Example:
LONG   1 XYZ 85 PUT   out-of-money at the lowest strike
SHORT 1 XYZ 90 PUT   out-of-the-money
SHORT 1 XYZ 100 PUT in-the-money
LONG   1 XYZ 105 PUT deeper in-the-money

In all circumstances the maximum loss is limited to the net debit paid assuming the distances between all four strikes prices are equal. In this illustration we chose to make the profit zone wider and risk an additional $500 for a higher probability of profit. The maximum loss would occur should the underlying be above the highest long put strike at expiration or at or below the lowest long put strike.   To risk only the debit, keep same distance between all the strikes.

LONG CALL BUTTERFLY

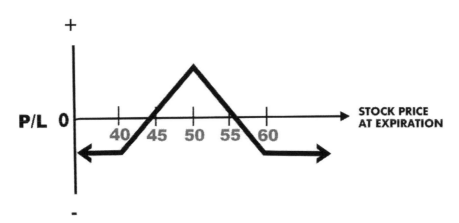

LONG CALL BUTTERFLY

Description: A combination trade consisting of two short CALLS at a middle strike - and one long call *each* at a lower and upper strike. Maximum profit requires the underlying to be at the short CALLS strike at expiration. The risk-reward can be adjusted by widening or narrowing the 'profitable pyramid' portion of the trade; the 'wings' should be equidistant from the middle strike.

Example:
LONG   1 XYZ 40 CALL (in-the-money)
SHORT 2 XYZ 50 CALLS   (at-the-money)
LONG   1 XYZ 60 CALL (out-of-the-money)

At expiration if the underlying is below all the strikes all the options would expire worthless; if above the strikes – all the options would be in-the-money and exercised with no profit. The maximum loss is the premium paid to initiate the trade. To win this one, the investor has to predict the price and time of the underlying; it is an aggressive trade in that respect.

SHORT CALL BUTTERFLY

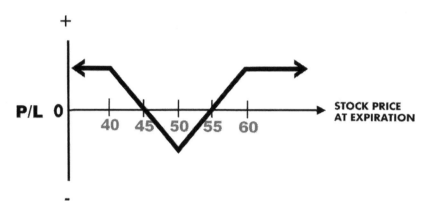

SHORT CALL BUTTERFLY

Description: The SHORT CALL BUTTERFLY is a combination with two long CALLS at the middle strike, and then a short CALL each and the upper and lower strike, usually equidistant from the middle. Maximum profit requires the underlying to be at the short CALLS strike at expiration. The risk-reward can be adjusted by widening or narrowing the 'profitable pyramid' portion of the trade; the 'wings' should be equidistant from the middle strike.

Example:
SHORT 1 XYZ 40 CALL (in-the-money)
LONG   2 XYZ 50 CALLS   (at-the-money)
SHORT 1 XYZ 60 CALL (out-of-the-money)

Maximum loss would be if the underlying is at the middle strike at expiration; maximum profit if the underlying at expiration is outside the 'wings'. This is an aggressive trade; the investor is depending on a significant move in the underlying in *either* direction. IV% has a small positive correlation to the trade, but not enough to be a major part of this strategy. Time-decay impact is negative. There is assignment risk and that can be an significant interference to this trade. Normally it is optimal for in the money options to be assigned just before expiration (the assumption is that you would exit the trade prior to expiration(, but they can be assigned at any time. Rating: very aggressive (risky).

LONG PUT BUTTERFLY

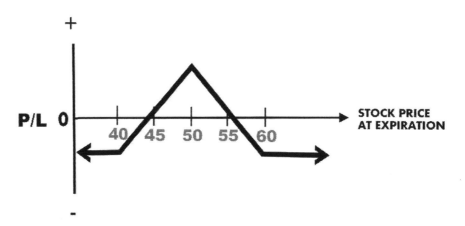

LONG PUT BUTTERFLY

Description: The LONG PUT BUTTERFLY is a combination trade consisting of two short PUT at a middle strike - and one long PUT *each* at a lower and upper strike. Maximum profit requires the underlying to be at the short middle CALLS strike at expiration. The risk-reward can be adjusted by widening or narrowing the 'profitable pyramid' portion of the trade; the 'wings' should be equidistant from the middle strike.

Example:
LONG 1 XYZ 40 PUT (out-of-the-money)
SHORT 2 XYZ 50 PUTS (at-the-money)
LONG 1 XYZ 60 PUT (in-the-money)

At expiration if the underlying is below all the strikes all the options would expire in-the-money. There is assignment risk with this trade, though not likely until a day before expiration date. If the underlying is above the strikes at expiration, all the options expire worthless. Maximum loss is the premium paid to initiate the trade. This is an aggressive trade since the investor has to pin both the price and timing to win. Comparable position is the LONG CALL BUTTERFLY.

SHORT PUT BUTTERFLY

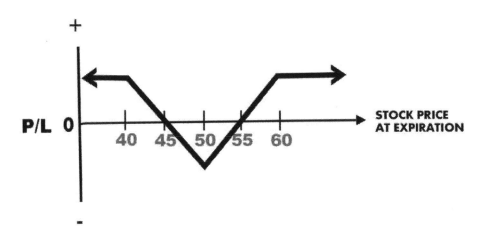

SHORT PUT BUTTERFLY

Description: The SHORT PUT BUTTERFLY is a combination trade consisting of two long PUTS at a middle strike - and one short PUT *each* at a lower and upper strike. Maximum profit requires the underlying to be outside the wings (40 & 60) at expiration. The risk-reward can be adjusted by widening or narrowing the 'wings' of the trade; the 'wings' should be equidistant from the middle strike.

Example:
SHORT 1 XYZ 40 PUT
LONG 2 XYZ 50 PUTS
SHORT 1 XYZ 60 PUT

All else being equal the SHORT CALL BUTTERFLY and the SHORT PUT BUTTERFLY would have the same payoff at expiration. There is assignment risk to this trade, but not likely until day before expiration. Maximum loss is with the underlying at the middle strike at expiration. There is a positive IV% correlation but not enough to make this trade a volatility play. Time-decay on the trade is positive is the body is at-the-money, and negative is the body is out-of-the-money. Comparable position is the SHORT CALL BUTTERFLY.

23 THE CALENDAR SPREAD

CALENDAR CALL SPREAD

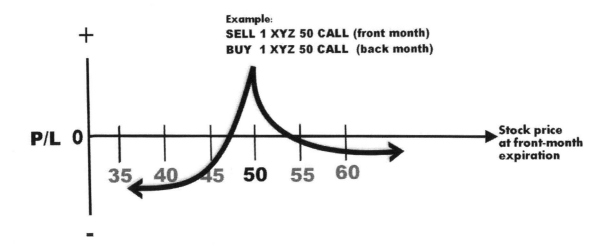

Example:
SELL 1 XYZ 50 CALL (front month)
BUY 1 XYZ 50 CALL (back month)

Description: Sell a CALL in front month with about 30 days until expiration, and buy a CALL at the same strike in the next month out. (SAME strike calendar spreads are called horizontal, using a higher strike would make this a diagonal spread). Notice the chart shows P/L at the expiration of the front month option.

The outlook at placing this trade is a steady to slightly bearish move in the underlying. At expiration of the front month, the trader can liquidate the back month CALL, or some traders look at this trade as a way to purchase the back month CALL at a reduced price; the latter is more often the objective. If this strategy works, the underlying is at or below the front strike and this front month option expires worthless, and the trader might keep the back month option to hold for gains as the underlying rises.

Increasing volatility (IV%) would have the back month increasing faster than the front month (all else being equal). Time-decay works in favor of this trade as the front month has a short time until expiration.

This CALENDAR CALL SPREAD is among the simplest configurations of CALENDAR SPREADS. Since various strikes can be used and they can be many short and long combinations for both horizontal and diagonal spreads – there are many combinations possible. Quick advice to beginners is do NOT use CALENDAR SPREADS; the nuance of various types of calendar spreads can be complex. For these reasons, this is the only calendar spread illustration in this book.

ABOUT THE AUTHOR

For over 25 years, Don A. Singletary through his company Sing Systems - was a private consultant to train and assist corporations to setup and evaluate hedge plans using computer option modeling for their risk management plans. He has written option trading articles for *Futures* and *Stocks & Commodities magazines*, and now publishes an option trading blog at OptionsExposed.net as well as writing books on investing - and conducting training classes for online stock & commodity option traders.

I sincerely thank you for your purchase and reading my book. I am always open to comments to help me make improvements and add new information in future editions. I publish additional information to help educate option traders on my website at **OptionsExposed.net** Please join me there for Q&A and more trading tips. Or you may contact me via email at **Don@WriteThisDown.com**

Go to page 177 NOW – and download the free PDF **3 Strategies That Work So Well the Pro's Try to Sell Them to You**. (It's free to those who have purchased this book). Send me an email with 'Bonus' in the subject -and I'll send it to you immediately –absolutely free.

Thank you and good luck-

Don A. Singletary

INDEX

SPECIAL BONUS CHAPTER
3 Strategies That Work So Well the Pro's
Try to Sell Them to You

FREE DOWNLOAD   SPECIAL BONUS CHAPTER

Just email me and put "BONUS" in the subject line and include a message if you like; I read them all and your comments and suggestions are welcomed.

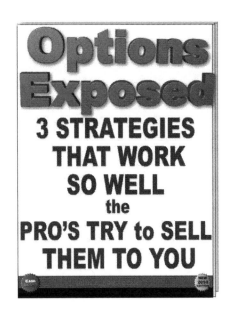

Don@WriteThisDown.com   "BONUS" in subject line

Thank you for purchasing the Options Exposed Playbook. As promised, you are entitled to a free 43 page PDF document that has *excerpts* from my best-selling eBook about "**3 Strategies That Work So Well the Pro's Try to Sell Them to You**".

Please visit my Options Exposed Blog at:

OptionsExposed.net/blog

to read more free, helpful hints on trading options and the psychology of trading them.

I offer this Special Bonus Chapter in PDF format so it can include many URL / live internet links to helpful information on option trading. Of course you may print it out if you like.

Thank you.

Made in the USA
Middletown, DE
06 September 2017